PINNACLE

PINNACLE
THE LOST PARADISE
OF RASTA

BY BILL "BLADE" HOWELL
WITH HÉLÈNE LEE

EDITED BY INGRID HOWELL

BROOKLYN, NEW YORK

Published by Akashic Books
©2024 Bill Howell and Hélène Lee
All rights reserved

ISBN: 978-1-63614-172-5
Library of Congress Control Number: 2023949549
First printing

Map of Jamaica (opposite) from 1962, modified with Pinnacle location by Akashic Books. Perry-Castañeda Library Map Collection, University of Texas at Austin.

Akashic Books
Instagram, X, Facebook: AkashicBooks
info@akashicbooks.com
www.akashicbooks.com

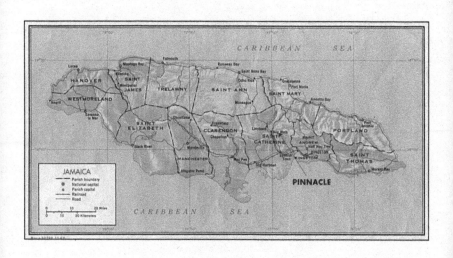

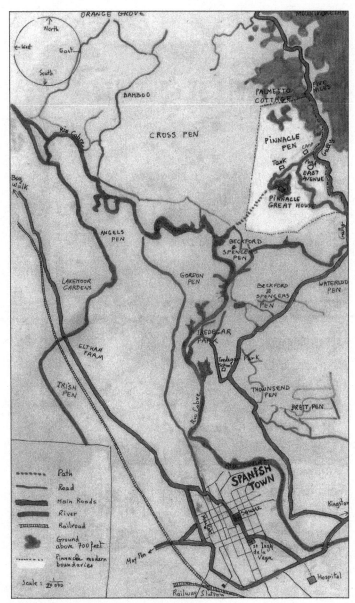

Spanish Town and the Pinnacle compound (in white).

TABLE OF CONTENTS

Introduction *11*

PART I: THE BIRTH OF RASTA
Percy *17*
Rastafari & Marcus Garvey *27*
1934: Red, Gold, and Green on Trial *33*
Tenneth Bent, the First Rasta Queen *37*
The 1938 Labor Rebellion *47*

PART II: PINNACLE
A Strategic Location *57*
The Neighborhood *63*
An Unsung Hero *67*
A New Era: 1946–1954 *77*
Water *81*
Pinnacle Productions *85*
Administration *93*
Education *99*
Health *105*
Diet and Dress Code *109*
Reasoning *113*
In the Lion's Den *121*

A Child's Paradise *125*
Entertainment *131*
Mystic *135*
Hurricane Charley *143*
Ganja *145*

PART III: BABYLON SYSTEM
Shakedowns *151*
The 1954 Ganja Raid *157*
Dark Years *163*
Not an Ordinary Kind of Man *173*

PART IV: HIGHER GROUND
Food for Thought *181*
The Search for God *193*
Highlight of My Life *197*

Afterword *201*

Dedication *204*
Acknowledgments *205*

INTRODUCTION

||||||||||||||||||||||||||||||||||||||||||||||||||||||||||||||||||||||||||

My very first memory is a bright and sunny day in 1944. I was only two years and some months old, but the images are still fresh in my mind. It was early morning, and a group of men and women were walking down a narrow path leading from Pinnacle, our home on the plateau, to Spanish Town, the old Jamaican capital on the coast. The path was rocky and precipitous, with thick bushes on either side. My nanny, Ethlyn Niklass, carried me in her arms, occasionally handing me to others in the party. My older brother Monty was five and hanging onto her skirt tail. It was a joyous time; people were singing, you could feel the unity. I remember crossing the Rio Cobre. We did not go around to the bridge. Instead, we took a shortcut across the river, since at that time of year the water was low. I can still see the women taking off their shoes . . . It was the first time I'd been away from the house; everything was new to my eyes.

When we got to our destination, which was the

courthouse complex, I couldn't believe my eyes. I had never seen such big buildings. But what overwhelmed me the most was the size of the crowd that had gathered there—hundreds of people.

Later in life, when people talked about that day, I would share my memories. My brother would say, "No, Billy, you can't remember, you were too young!" But I remember; I was there.

We were standing in the crowd in front of the tall buildings, singing our songs, and at one point all hell broke loose. Everyone was pointing at something above our heads, screaming, "See 'im deh! See 'im deh!" A man was crossing a catwalk leading from one building of the courthouse to the next, and for a few seconds he was in full view of the crowd below. Even as I watched, I had no idea what was causing all the excitement. Who was that person up there?

I had only faint memories of my father; he'd been in jail for most of my young life. And although I did not know the reason for all the commotion, somehow I knew that it was because of him. I realized that all these people were there just for this man, Leonard Percival Howell.

A few months earlier, my mother, Tenneth Bent-Howell, had died under mysterious circumstances. The colonial authorities, who were looking for any pretext to get rid of my father and his community of followers, had accused him of murdering his beloved wife, my mother. Dada had been in jail since then, and on that day in March 1944, the court was having its first hearing.

Fortunately, my father was acquitted and he came home. On April 6, 1944, the main Jamaican newspaper, the *Daily Gleaner*, wrote, "The attorney general entered a *nolle prosequi* in the manslaughter charge against Leonard Howell, head of the cult that holds out at 'Pinnacle,' St. Catherine, and a crowd of his followers escorted their leader back to his home."

Who was this man, my father, Leonard Percival Howell? What was this "cult" he created? Why was he persecuted, jailed, dispossessed, and eventually denied a place in history?

The story of my father, the founder of the Rasta movement, is *still* a mystery, even to the millions across the globe who claim his heritage. Researchers have started showing interest in Pinnacle, the first Rasta commune, but there are no firsthand accounts of our life there, no basic information which could contribute to a serious discussion of the nature of the movement.

It seems that it is left to me, a son of Leonard P. Howell, born and raised at Pinnacle, to tell the true story.

PART I
THE BIRTH OF RASTA

Leonard Percival Howell, circa 1936.

PERCY

||||||||||||||||||||||||||||||||||||||||||||||||||||||||||||||||||||||||||||||||||||||

My father never talked much about his past. He would talk about New York or Africa or France, and we never doubted that he knew all those places. But he never revealed much about his personal life there; we did not ask either. I was a child, and there was too much happening in my life. In recent years, however, my memories have started haunting me; and coupled with the research I have done, facts are beginning to emerge.

Leonard Percival Howell was born on June 16, 1898, in the remote village of Red Lands in the parish of Clarendon, Jamaica (then a British colony). He was the first child of Charles Theophilus and Clementina Howell, a peasant family of some means. At the end of his life, through hard work and sober living, Charles Howell had acquired numerous acres of land and was a respected elder of the local church.

I have personally researched the Howell family lineage back to our great-great-great-grandfather, Richard Howell, and his wife, Sarah Howell, who was born in 1794 and died on October 13, 1894. I am of the fifth generation of Jamaican Howells.

My grandparents on both sides of my family worked hard to acquire sizable plots of land for their children to inherit. Alas, that wasn't to be for my parents, or for us, their legacy.

Declaration of intention to become a citizen of the United States of America (May 1924). As a slight, Leonard Howell's height is entered incorrectly.

* * *

Growing up, my siblings and I called my father "Dada," but in his own youth he was known as "Percy," an abbreviation of his middle name. When Dada became a thought leader, his followers and the people at Pinnacle called him "Counselor," "Prince Regent," or simply "Mr. Howell." Later, people outside of Pinnacle would refer to him as "Gong," which was short for his pen name, Gangun Guru Maragh or G.G. Maragh. But no one at Pinnacle ever called or referred to him in that way. For reasons one can only guess at, Mortimer Planno, an intelligent Rasta leader and Bob Marley's mentor, later took to calling the singer "Little Gong," and people say that is why Bob named his record company "Tuff Gong." But when you hear someone refer to my father as "Gong," you know that this person is not a Howellite.

My father's childhood nickname, Percy, was first published in the Jamaican press in 1915 in a controversial investigation: the Rodney case. A murder had taken place in Red Lands, next door to Dada's childhood home. The victim was a neighbor and the police suspected one of my father's relatives, Edward Rodney, of committing the crime. Dada had seen Rodney going into the lady's house on that same afternoon, and although he was a teenager, the police detained and interrogated him for three days in the local jail. They wanted him to testify against his relative, but the family did not agree with the mandate. Yet in the end, Dada had no choice but to appear in court.

Rodney had an excellent attorney, J.A.G. Smith, "the lawyer of the poor," who was the first Black attorney in Jamaica, and who also happened to come from the same region. Under Smith's guidance, my father gave a very prudent and straightforward testimony. He was introduced as a fourteen-year-old boy (he had just turned seventeen), but his self-assurance impressed the crowd and drew a smile from the judge. Edward Rodney was found guilty and condemned to death, but J.A.G. Smith, thanks to the "circumstantial nature of the evidence" given by the boy, was able to appeal to the Privy Council in London and the sentence was reversed.

Rodney was eventually released, though when he came out of jail, he was bitter and angry. He threatened people, and his primary target was Percy, who lived next door. Rodney's aggressive attitude soon brought him before the court again. Something ugly was bound to happen, so my grandmother decided that the boy had better leave. At the age of nineteen, my father went into exile, leaving Jamaica, its beautiful hills, and its brutal police.

We seldom went to the parish of Clarendon, and I do not know much about my father's time living there. I do remember going there on a couple of occasions when I was very young—maybe five years old. What sticks in my mind is that we took the train—a dramatic event for me; it was the first time I had taken this fancy locomotive with gaslights. We got off at

May Pen and caught a taxi from there. You could not drive up to the house my father had inhabited, so we had to walk up a steep, steep hill.

When my father left Jamaica at the end of 1917, World War I was in full swing. It is believed that, like thousands of men in Jamaica and other British territories, Dada enrolled in some service to help his "Mother Country England fight the evil Germans for the freedom of the world"—as all Jamaicans were supposed to believe. He often told us stories of the slaughter, of the terrible experiences these Black soldiers endured in World War I, especially South Africans who were not allowed to carry guns even though they were serving on the front line as soldiers, cooks, and corpsmen. Yet no document has ever emerged confirming Leonard Howell's participation in the ranks of the British army.

What the US immigration archives do confirm are my father's many trips on US Army ships, which took him twice around the globe. In a police hearing in 1932, he described some of the places he visited:

> *I was sent back in 1918 to Colón, Panama, by the Jamaican government on a boat of the United Fruit Co. to proceed to Canada . . . I remained in Colón a short while and joined the US Army Transport Service as a cook, and during the fall of 1918 I went to San Francisco. From San Francisco, I went to the Philippine Islands and to Vladivostok, Siberia, to take a*

New York State Prison,
Auburn, N. Y.
May 19, 1932.

830/338

REPORT OF PRELIMINARY EXAMINATION accorded the alien LEONARD HOWELL, place and date above noted, in the English language, by Immigrant Inspector Michael J. Costello, examining officer and stenographer:

Q What is your full and correct name?
A LEONARD HOWELL, No. 44816.
Q Were you ever known by any other name?
A Yes, JOSEPH LEONARD.
Q When and where were you born, and of what country are you a citizen?
A I was born July 16, 1908, in Mohoe Hill, Jamaica, B. W. I., which is near Kingston, Jamaica, B.W.I. I am a citizen of the British West Indies.
Q What are your age, race, sex, occupation and religion?
A 31 years; African black; male; cook; Protestant (Church of England).
Q When, where and in what manner did you enter the U. S.?
A I first entered the U. S. during May, 1918, at New York, N. Y. as a passenger on a boat of the United Fruit Co. from Kingston, Jamaica. I do not remember the name of the ship. I paid a head tax at that time.
Q Are you married or single?
A I was married but I am now separated. I married Myra Wilson, a native of the B.W.I., in Panama during 1922. I received a legal separation from her in 1925 in New York City. I do not know her present address.
Q What are the names, birthplaces and present addresses of your parents?
A My father, Charles Howell, and mother, Clementine Bennett, were both born in Mohoe Hill, Jamaica, B.W.I., and are now both dead. They were never in the U.S. and were citizens of the B.W.I.
Q What relatives have you in the U. S.?
A Only a cousin, Levine Palmer; her last known address to me was 2326 - 7th Ave., New York City.
Q What relatives have you abroad?
A Two brothers, Osbert and Leslie Howell; two aunts, Sarah and Jane Bennett, all in the village of Mohoe Hill, Jamaica, B.W.I.
Q What schools and churches did you attend abroad?
A St. Gregory's School and St. Gregory's Church, Mohoe Hill, Jamaica, B.W.I. I think I was baptized in that church when I was a baby.
Q Have you a birth certificate or any other document of nationality?
A No. (NOTE: Letter written by alien for birth certificate.)
Q By whom were you last employed in the B.W.I.?
A I was never employed there.
Q Were you ever refused admission to, or deported from, the U. S.?
A No.
Q Were you ever confined in any hospital or other like institution?
A No.
Q Were you ever a public charge?
A No.
Q How many times have you been arrested?
A Twice. I was first arrested during 1924 for burglary. At that time I lived at 66 W. 131st St., New York City, and I had a roomer there who owed me $14. room rent; he didn't pay me so I took a suitcase and a violin that he had for security. He didn't show up with the money to pay for the room rent, so I took the suitcase and violin and pawned them for $14. He came around later and wanted his suitcase and violin and I told him that I pawned them and gave him the ticket and then he

830/338   (1)   Page____   EXHIBIT "A"

Above and right: L.P. Howell's deposition during his imprisonment in the Auburn Correctional Facility, May 1932 (deportation file).

swore out a warrant for my arrest. The case was dismissed in court, and he paid the $14. to get his possession out of pawn. I was next arrested on November 19 or 20, 1930 for burglary, 3rd degree, grand larceny 2nd degree and receiving stolen property in New York City. I was hired by a racketeer in New York by the name of Feltman to go over to Long Island to get some rugs and other household furnishings and merchandise, and on the way back I was stopped by the police in New York. They investigated and found that this was stolen property that I had and they put me under arrest. I did not know this property was stolen. Feltman paid me $10. to bring it over to New York. I was convicted of 3rd degree burglary, grand larceny 2nd degree and receiving stolen property in Queens County Court, Long Island City, NY on January 16, 1931, and received a sentence of from two to four years.

Q Were you guilty of these offenses?
A No.
Q Do you read and write?
A Yes. (Tested, R&W English)
Q Did you ever try to become a citizen of the U. S.?
A Yes, I took out first papers in June, 1924 in New York City. The papers are now with my common-law wife, Louise Smith, Apt. 6, 217 W. 121st St., New York City.
Q When and where did you last enter the United States?
A I last entered the United States on or about August 25, 1929, after a visit of 1½ months in Montreal, Canada. I entered the U. S. at Niagara Falls, N. Y. via bridge; I was driving a Buick convertible coupe at the time.
Q With whom did you visit while in Montreal?
A A friend of mine from the B.W.I., John McNeil, St. Catherine St., West, Montreal, Canada. I travelled from Montreal to Toronto, Canada, and then came through Niagara Falls, N. Y.
Q Were you at that time examined and admitted to the U.S. by an immigration officer?
A Yes; he asked me where I was born, how long I had lived in the U. S. and how long I had been in Canada on this trip. I told him I was born in Jamaica, B.W.I. and that I was legally admitted to the U. S. in 1918 and that I had been in Canada about 1½ months.
Q Where have you been employed since your entry into the U. S.?
A Until about the end of 1923 I was employed in the Army Transport Service, War Department, foot of 59th St., Brooklyn, N. Y. on various vessels; USS "Logan", "Madawaska", "Edgemore", "Sherman", "Grant". I travelled all over; to China and Japan and around the world twice. xxxxxxxxxx
Q Where have you been employed since 1923?
A I was employed by Mr. Tedeschi, a builder, 471 Crescent St., Astoria, L. I.; for 3 years; Burkhard & Disinni, Builders, Richmond Hill, L. I., 1½ years; Mueller & Young, Builders, Woodhaven Blvd., Jamaica, L. I. - 4 or 5 months; then I went into business for myself at 113 W. 136th St., New York City, where I operated a tea room.
Q When do you expect to be released from this prison?
A About July 1, 1932.
Q Do you own any property or have you a bank account?
A No. I own some restaurant equipment valued at about $800. located at 113 W. 136th St., New York City.
Q Have you anything else to say?   A. No.

PERSONAL DESCRIPTION: Height, 5'9"; weight, 163 lbs.; brown eyes; black hair; oval face; large nose and mouth. Cross scar back of right hand.

DISMISSED.

Michael J. Costello,
Immigrant Inspector.   EXHIBIT "A"

830/338   Page____

23

*load of Czechoslovak soldiers to Trieste, Italy,
and from there I came back to New York and
was sent by the War Department to San Francisco to join the USS* Grant *which was detailed
to take Secretary of War Weeks to Honolulu
and back; when I went back, I went on the
USS* Edgemore, *on which I worked until 1923,
when I was discharged in New York.*

Immigration documents confirm this story as well.

When the war ended, my father settled in the United States, where he lived until 1932, primarily in New York. In the fabulous Black mecca of the roaring twenties, he met and exchanged ideas with Black intellectual leaders of the time: Jomo Kenyatta, Kwame Nkrumah, Nnamdi Azikiwe, George Padmore, and, of course, his compatriot Marcus Garvey, the most renowned among them, whom he knew very well.

My father always talked about New York. He mentioned Harlem, Hoboken (New Jersey), and Astoria (Queens), where he spent most of his time. In the 1932 police hearing, he claimed he was employed by three different building contractors on Long Island over the span of five years. He stated that in 1928, "I went into business for myself at 113 West 136th Street, New York City, where I operated a tearoom . . . I own some restaurant equipment valued at about $800."

He visited other cities, including San Francisco,

Baltimore, and Chicago, but I don't think he stayed long in any of those places.

Immigration archives show that in 1922 in Colón, Panama, he married Myra Wilson, a Jamaican seamstress, and divorced her in 1925 in New York—though I never heard my father mention her. The subject of his personal life was rarely talked about. It is quite possible he had other children in the States or in Panama; I only know of those who were born after his return to Jamaica.

New York in 1929 was, like most industrial cities in the world, shaken by the Great Depression. My father, who had just opened the tearoom in Harlem, was most likely feeling the blow. One of his neighbors on 136th Street was Casper Holstein, the city's biggest *Bolita* King of the times, and his number runners were clients of my father's shop. But in 1928, Holstein had ceased operations after having been abducted for several days by a gang, and the number runners were gone. Everyone's pockets were empty, and when someone appeared with a job offer, questions were usually not asked.

My father took on an additional job with a man named Feltman, who offered to pay him ten dollars to drive a truck from Long Island to New York City. On the evening of November 19, 1930, while en route to the city, my father was stopped by police and it was discovered that the rugs and furniture in the truck were stolen. My father was soon convicted of receiving stolen goods and complicity in a burglary. He was sent to the Sing Sing Correctional Facility in Ossining, New York, and later transferred to the Auburn Correctional Facility, before finally being released in 1932.

He arrived in Jamaica on November 18, 1932, on the SS *Sixaola* of the United Fruit Co.

This information came as a shock to me. I cannot imagine my righteous father committing a crime of that nature—he obviously took the rap for someone else. Why weren't the real criminals prosecuted? Justice in America was, and in many cases still is, tough for the Black man. Was not the great Marcus Garvey himself deported on the mere "evidence" of an empty envelope? At the height of the Great Depression, immigration was at a standstill and US officials were deporting any alien they could lay their hands on.

The files I've unearthed reveal that the police officer who questioned my father did not mention in his report that Dada had been employed by the US Army Transport for five years, which would have made him ineligible for deportation. This injustice was to have a major impact on my father's life.

RASTAFARI &
MARCUS GARVEY

||||||||||||||||||||||||||||||||||||||||||||||||||||||||||||||||||||||||||||||||||||||||||||||

I am not an expert in religion, though I have learned that certain people cannot believe in something unless it takes a religious form.

On November 2, 1930, shortly before my father's arrest in New York, His Imperial Majesty Haile Selassie I of Ethiopia was crowned King of Kings and Lord of Lords, Conquering Lion of the Tribe of Judah. My father was a Christian who knew the Bible inside and out, and he remembered a prophecy from the Book of Revelation:

> *And I saw a strong angel proclaiming in a loud voice, "Who is worthy to open the Book, and to release the seals thereof?" . . . And one of the elders saith unto me, "Weep not: behold, the Lion of Judah, the root of David, hath prevailed to open the Book and to lose the seven spirits of God sent forth into all the Earth."*

A new king had come to all the "Ethiopians" of the world, and this man was of a divine lineage. He would lead the Black people to redemption, and free Africa. Dada was soon a changed man.

My father's idea was to add a religious element to Marcus Garvey's basic message of African independence. "This Christian god that you are worshiping is not *your* god," my father would say. Although Christian values were part of his belief system, Dada decided to make a break from the Christian interpretation of the Bible and extend the idea of divinity to this new king. He not only told the people, he *showed* them. He knew all the relevant Bible verses.

At a trial in Morant Bay in 1934, when the judge asked Robert Hinds, one of my father's lieutenants, "Who is God?" Hinds answered, "The emperor."

"Why do you believe that?"

"Because Mr. Howell told me so."

"So, he just tells you and you believe?"

"No, he showed us in the Bible that what he says is true."

People used to argue that Garvey started the Rasta movement. In reality, Garvey didn't want to have anything to do with Rasta. He was a pious Christian Methodist and had no desire to change his faith; in fact, he wanted his movement to stay clear of religion.

He told my father on several occasions not to preach his blanket nonsense at any of his—Garvey's—meetings. And yet, these two men respected each other and remained personal friends. There is no doubt that my father was influenced by Marcus Garvey, having attended many of the man's conventions in New York and seen that you can open people's minds just by talking to them. He saw what wonders the Word can do.

Many incorrectly believe that it was Garvey who uttered the famous prophecy, "Look to Africa, where a Black man shall be crowned, in him you will find the Redeemer." But those words were spoken by the Reverend James Morris Webb in 1921. I remember hearing people say that Rasta was Garvey's brainchild; I would refute that and tell them what I knew, but they would often say things like, "Who's Leonard Howell? Nobody here knows him!" and claim that my father had jumped on Garvey's ideas and brought people up to Pinnacle to fool them into believing *he* was God. That always filled me with resentment, and led to many fierce arguments.

Why did my father choose Ras Tafari Makonnen—Emperor Haile Selassie I—as his new inspiration, and eventually declare him a "Living God"?

Ethiopia once cast, and in some ways still casts, a powerful image. One must remember that in 1930, it was the only independent nation in all of Africa that was neither a colony nor a puppet state. In those days, the entire continent was enslaved by five European powers; the minerals belonged to non-Africans, the people were controlled by non-Africans. And yet

Ethiopia had been independent from foreign dominion for thousands of years. In 1896, when the Italians tried to conquer the land, Ethiopians fought back and triumphed under the guidance of Negus Menelik. So, when Ras Tafari was crowned emperor, my father declared, "Believe in that man who's going to change the Black race!"

Some would say, "Well, Garvey started the Black Redemption process." That's fine; my father told me that he and Garvey had basically the same message: fighting against injustice. But feeling the need to broaden the appeal of that message, Dada contended that the emperor was the Living God—and this definitely drew people in.

When my father started to preach on street corners in Kingston and St. Thomas, most of those who gathered around were small farmers, poor people, and struggling single mothers. It was not the merchants and the upper class. Years later, the rebellious sons of the gentry, attracted to the Rasta way of life, adopted the look and language, and there was a reawakening of Rasta in Kingston. But in the beginning, Dada's movement took root on the very lowest level of Jamaican society. He saw the terrible conditions poor people were enduring and decided that something must be done to change their situation.

The movement Dada started was one of the first nonviolent campaigns against British colonial rule—before Mahatma Gandhi (who started his campaign in India in the 1940s), and before Martin Luther King

Jr. (who started in the US in the 1950s). As early as 1932, my father was nonviolently protesting against Great Britain, the greatest superpower on earth at that time. His vision was one of self-reliance—poor people working together to build a society of their own—and this is what he started to preach.

In the beginning, he met with very little success. He was ridiculed on the street, even by Garvey, who had returned from the US five years earlier and was trying to rebuild his glorious Universal Negro Improvement Association (UNIA). Garvey's followers chased my father from the steps of the Coke Chapel in Kingston, which they considered to be the private speaking ground of their leader.

1934: RED, GOLD, AND GREEN ON TRIAL

‖‖

S lavery was abolished in Jamaica in 1834, and in the subsequent years there were hundreds of thousands of unemployed, formerly enslaved Black people roaming the island trying to survive. Despite this viable labor pool, the planters and larger sugar estate owners somehow managed to convince the colonial government that they needed a new and cheaper workforce, and so the British looked to India, China, and Africa to fill the gap. In 1845, they began to ship indentured servants from those lands to Jamaica and all throughout the British West Indian colonies. Thirty-two thousand Indian indentured workers arrived in Jamaica in May of 1845 alone; the indentured servitude policy would last into the early part of the twentieth century.

When my father began preaching on street corners in Kingston, he was immediately perceived as "seditious" by the authorities, and he became a target for police harassment. So after a while, he decided to move to St. Thomas, an eastern parish. St. Thomas was sugarcane country, still very rural, with lots of large and small farms, all owned and run by white colonial planters.

When Dada arrived in St. Thomas, his organization, which he had named the Ethiopian Salvation Society, went into overdrive. A proper rule book with bylaws was printed and widely distributed among workers, the unemployed, and indentured servants. My father told his new followers to give all of their allegiance, love, respect, and faith to this young king, Ras Tafari Makonnen, who had been crowned in Ethiopia in 1930. He was the true sign of change for Black people, who had been exploited and abused for the last four hundred years. Dada advised poor people to start working together to build their own society right here on the island: "Jamaica is as much yours as any English person's. We paid for it with the blood of our ancestors. Arise and shine, for the light has come and the glory of the Living God is upon you!"

My father would quote the Bible but also other religious books, because he liked to study all kinds of philosophies. He preached "peace and love" long before the American hippies in the 1960s claimed that phrase. Our usual greeting was, "Peace and love, Brother So-and-so . . ." "Peace and love, my sister." Our banner was inspired by the very first Ethiopian tri-pennant flag, from before the Anglo-Ethiopian Treaty of 1897. The three colors, from top to bottom, were red, yellow (or gold), and green. On October 6, 1897, the Ethiopian government changed their flag to what it remains today: green on top and red on the bottom, with yellow in the middle.

My father used those original pennant colors of the Ethiopian nation to signify the birth of something new, yet still as old as the Ethiopian nation. It has been suggested that if he had put the green stripe on top, with yellow and red below, he could have been arrested for raising a foreign flag in a British colony; he could have been sentenced to a long prison term, possibly even death. But this was not the rationale he gave me. He wanted to show respect to the Ethiopian people, who had very strict laws governing their flag. In Ethiopia, you could be incarcerated for messing with the flag. So the red, gold, and green banner started to fly over Kingston and St. Thomas, and soon spread to other Jamaican parishes.

It did not take long for the authorities to react. On February 1, 1934, the *Daily Gleaner* carried the headline, "Howell Committed to Stand Trial for Sedition." My father and his codefendants, Robert Hinds and Osmond Shaw, had been speaking at several meetings in St. Thomas, and police informers had taken notes on what they said.

The trial lasted three days and was extensively covered in the national newspapers. The people and the government of Jamaica had discovered a daring new movement, based on the belief that Emperor Haile Selassie I was the messiah returned to earth. Jamaican journalists coined a name for the group: the "Ras Tafarites," or "Rastas."

My father was found guilty of sedition and sentenced to prison for two years of hard labor; Robert Hinds, one of my father's earliest followers, got one year.

I don't know the whole story there, whether they had a falling-out or what, but only Shaw later lived at Pinnacle.

The sole mention I ever heard of a man named Joseph Hibbert was from Brother Delahaie, a Kingston man who moved to Pinnacle. My father never mentioned Hinds nor Hibbert, but somehow history has incorporated them, along with Shaw, as among the founding fathers of Rasta.

TENNETH BENT,
THE FIRST RASTA QUEEN

||||||||||||||||||||||||||||||||||||||||||||||||||||||||||||||||||||||||||||||||||

Among the many Jamaicans who had been following the 1934 trial and contemplating my father's speeches was a young woman of twenty-two who was destined to play an important role in his life. My mother would soon become his secretary, his second-in-command, and the only other person to help with funding for the purchase of Pinnacle. And she ran all his affairs while he was in jail, prison, and the Bellevue psychiatric hospital.

Tenneth Bent was born on March 7, 1912, in Southfields, St. Elizabeth. She came from a family of what we call "white Jamaicans" who were landowners with mixed origins (and fair skin)—mainly Scottish, Irish, German, Jewish, English (the former slave masters), and the unavoidable drop of African blood. She had moved to Kingston early in life to attend school; later she worked for the Machado Tobacco Company at the bottom of South Camp Road. She was a very bright, pretty, and promising young woman, and there was a rumor that she had been engaged to one of the Machado sons who was heir to the family's cigarette business and fortune.

Tenneth Bent-Howell, L.P. Howell's wife and Monty and Bill Howell's mother (circa 1937–1938).

I do not know how she met my father, but when she did, she fell in love with that tall, good-looking, charismatic Black man with broad shoulders, often dressed in a three-piece suit. He had returned from New York somewhat recently, still sporting the latest fashion, and his dreams of universal justice must have been intoxicating. He had a commanding presence and spoke perfect English in a deep, powerful voice. When he came out of prison, they had a short whirlwind romance and promptly married.

A photo of Emperor Selassie that L.P. Howell distributed throughout his life; a reproduction of the original which was badly damaged during the raids.

The
Promised Key
by
G. G. Maragh

Dr. Nnamdi Azikiwe
Editor of
The African Morning Post
HEAD OFFICE
Accra, Gold Coast.

The Promised Key was a small pamphlet
published by L.P. Howell in 1936 under the
pseudonym G.G. Maragh.

H. I. M.
the
EMPEROR HAILE SELASSIE

The Promised Key, original edition.

covered lion's manes were to be seen. In profression then were the solar note struck by the women who were heavily veiled and wore heavy cloaks.

His and Her Majesty King Alpha and Queen Omega the King of Kings drove to the Cathedral in a coach drawn by six white arab horses.

Queen Omega in a robe of silver and the escort on mules wearing lion's skin over their shoulders. Forming into procession on side the Cathedral.

King Ras Tafari and Queen Omega the Royal pair, the nearts and a line of Bishops and Priests entered, the guests rank obeisance.

King Alpha sitting on his Throne homage was done to him by the Bishops and Priests fulfilling the 21st Psalm.

The ceremony took 10 days from the second day to the eleventh day of November 1930.

King Alpha was presented with the orb spurs, and spears and many other mighty emblem of His High Office, Dignitaries of the world power presented King Alpha with the wealth of oceans.

The Emperor attended to most of his preparations for the reception of his thousands of guests himself, and day after day could be seen rushing about in his scarlet car seeing how the ordinary labourers were getting on with the new road he had ordered that the lawns he had laid down be attended to, and that the extension of the electric lights throughout the city were being hurried on.

THE FALSE RELIGON

All the churches religious system of today, claim to represent the Lord God of Israel; but with the Pope who is satan the devil, false organization, it is a hypocritical religious system that has three elements, first commercial political and ecclesiastical, to keep the people in ignorance of their wicked course.

Money power is the great bulwark of their organization; and they use the religious elements as a smoke screen to keep the people in ignorance of the truth.

The false teachers under the supervision of the Pope of Rome who is satan the devil. The agents of his speaking lies, in the churches, and let the people walk in darkness.

My dear readers you can see that all their foundations of the earth are out of course. Allow me to say that there is no throne for the Anglo Saxon white people, they must come

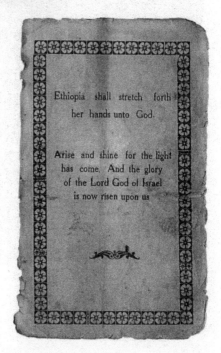

Ethiopia shall stretch forth
her hands unto God.

Arise and shine for the light
has come. And the glory
of the Lord God of Israel
is now risen upon us

The Promised Key, original edition.

the city of Samaria. She found out that her first teachers of denominations throughout the state or country of Samaria were false. Then she cried aloud unto the inhabitance of the city and said "Come see a man that told me all over I did" and is not a native of Samaria, but an Hebrew, is not this man the very Christ. Our cities of today are inhabited with the same qualities of people as it was in the case of Jesus and the woman of Samaria.

THE HEALING

The healing plough of the respository transplanted and rebuild our very soul and body without fail. The misery of the land is healed by fasting. King Alpha pick us up from out of the midst of the raging misery of the land and hide us from the raging wolves of the land into our Balm Yard. What is a Balm Yard? A Balm Yard is a holy place that is wholly consecrated to God Almighty for the cleansing and healing of the nations. Where only the holy spirit of God alone is allowed to do the Royal work of healing. Who does the balming work? Consecrated men and women that the holy spirit moves upon the blazing alter of their soul and endowed them with power that they command and handle the infirmities of the nations.

Have we any authority from King Alpha? Yes we are vessels of the divine honour. Have we any authority from the Lord? assuredly yes indeed, King Alpha signs for our destiny and gave us His supreme Affidavit for a trillion centuries after the end of eternal life.

BALM YARD

First and last every soul for admission must be believer in the power of King Ras Tafari the living God.

An admission fee must be paid in advance from four shillings up according to the power and duration of the miserable infirmities whereof one is afflicted. (Special Notice)

Sometime King Alpha have to proform special medical attention.

(ROYAL NOTICE)

King Alpha said Bands are not runned by Ministers, they are runned by the Priesthood not after the order of Aaron but strictly after the Royal Order of King Ras Tafari the King of Kings of Ethiopia.

Revivalists are not common people. If some individuals of the lower order in the dung heap happen to get into the fold by mistake he or she will soon get out and hung him or herself.

The Promised Key, original edition.

His Majesty Ras Tafari
King of Kings
King of Ethiopia and the Conquering Lion
Juda the Elect of God and Light of the
World.

The Promised Key, original edition.

* * *

Upon his release in 1936, my father started a bakery at 108 Princess Street in Kingston. It was an immediate success; the profits yielded a good income, which allowed Dada to continue preaching his ideas. In addition to the sales of a picture of the Prince Regent, Dada also published a book, *The Promised Key*, under an Indian pseudonym, "Gangunguru G.G. Maragh, Guru King of the Universe."

Dada was now gathering crowds in the hundreds in St. Thomas, despite it being a rural parish with limited means of news distribution; there were no local newspapers, radio and television stations, or telephones, just word of mouth—my father knew how to stir an audience.

One of the stories being circulated about my father after he started his new movement was that he could strike lightning. Electricity in those days was like magic to the Jamaican populace, and many people didn't have access to it; only a few really understood what it was. The truth of the story is that my father climbed an electric pole one afternoon and joined two wires together, using his fountain pen, and there was a huge spark. Whether he was simply giving a lesson in splicing wires or explaining how electricity worked, the effects were the same: it was mystifying and captivating, and some people thought it was the most miraculous thing they had ever seen. It convinced them that Leonard Howell was no ordinary person; he was a great man, a mystic!

There must have been a lot of gossip going around about Dada in order to bring hundreds of people together in one place. He told his audiences about Ras Tafari, the new King of Kings of the Black race. He explained that King George of England was not *their* king, so they should stop paying taxes to the colonial administration and start building their own society.

The planters and British authorities were outraged by my father's challenge to the status quo, while local churches felt threatened by his public condemnation of their cooperation with the oppressors. Soon the whole establishment—the churches, the planters, the government, and the police—decided to join forces to try to get rid of him once and for all. This dark-skinned Negro was playing God, and the story of him striking lightning was undoubtedly one of the pretexts invoked in 1938 to intern my father in a psychiatric hospital.

Telephone No.
VICTORIA 1582-3-4-5

BOX NO. 500,
PARLIAMENT STREET, B.O.
LONDON, S.W.1.

411/West Indies/B4b.

14th September 1938,

Dear Mr Woolley,

Reference your secret letter of 23.3.34;
Leonard HOWELL is now in communication with the
International African Service Bureau in London.
They have sent him two packets of literature
which he has not however received. His present
address appears to be 6 Sea Breeze Avenue, Windward
Road P.O., Bournemouth Garden, Kingston.

HOWELL has apparently started a movement
which he calls the African Salvation Union of
Jamaica. He describes it as an international
organisation pledged to support morally and financially
the continued independence, national integrity and
complete sovereignty of Africa.

I do not imagine that the movement is nearly
so important as HOWELL makes out, but you may like
to know of his connection with the African Service
Bureau.

Yours sincerely,

[signature]

Colonel Sir Vernon Kell.

C.C.Woolley, Esq., CMG., OBE. HE.
        Colonial Secretary,
        Jamaica.

Letter from Colonel Vernon Kell, founder of the London secret service (Box 500 was the address for MI5), to the Jamaican colonial secretary.

THE 1938 LABOR REBELLION

||||||||||||||||||||||||||||||||||||||||||||||||||||||||||||||||||||||||||||||||||||||||||||||

S ocial conditions among workers in St. Thomas were appalling, and revolt was brewing. The 1938 "revolution" was about to upset the colonial order. There has never been any tangible evidence linking my father to the 1938 upheaval, but the authorities believed him to be an instigator of trouble. They prohibited his meetings or sent hooligans to disrupt them. The year before, in January 1937, they had hired a gang of thugs and plainclothes policemen to attack an Ethiopian Christmas festival my father had organized. The Rastas were stoned, robbed, beaten, and terrorized, while police made no attempt to intervene or arrest the attackers. My father was eventually banned from St. Thomas.

The Kingston authorities were not eager to get him back, so they devised a new trick—they declared him insane. In February 1938, on the strength of a falsified medical report, he was committed to Bellevue.

While he was locked up there, the 1938 rebellion was still raging—strikes were spreading across the whole island. This would eventually play a role in the introduction of adult suffrage (1944) and Jamaican independence (1962). Later, historians would deny Dada's influence on the 1938 revolution, yet the movement had started right there at Serge Island, the St. Thomas sugar estate where he often spoke to large audiences.

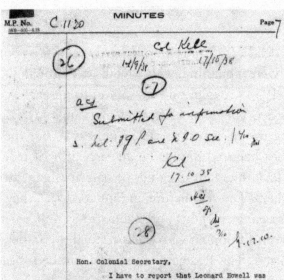

M.P. No. C 1120   MINUTES   Page 7

Hon. Colonial Secretary,

    I have to report that Leonard Howell was certified insane and sent to the Lunatic Asylum on the 15th February 1938 of which Institution he is still an inmate.

2.   His wife resides at No.6 Sea Breeze Avenue and I understand that letters addressed to Howell are opened by his wife who takes them to him at the Asylum. He reads them and instructs her what replies are to be sent. She conducts Howell's correspondence.

3.   Howell's followers have never heard of the Movement referred to in paragraph 2 of (26).

4.   Mrs. Howell received a letter sometime ago from the International African Service Bureau of London enquiring if her husband had received the literature sent him. The literature has not arrived, and

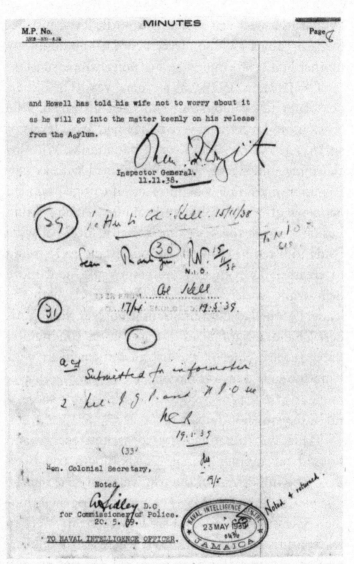

and Howell has told his wife not to worry about it
as he will go into the matter keenly on his release
from the Asylum.

Inspector General.
11.11.38.

Hon. Colonial Secretary,

Noted.

D.C.
for Commissioner of Police.
20. 5. 39.

TO NAVAL INTELLIGENCE OFFICER.

Above and left: Note from the inspector general informing the colonial secretary of the intelligence
gathered on L.P. Howell, in response to Colonel Vernon Kell's 1938 letter (Jamaican Archives,
Spanish Town).

* * *

Leonard Howell was released from Bellevue just before Christmas 1938, on December 20—no doubt my mother had been employing her powerful persuasion.

For Jamaica, 1939 was a crucial year. The old order of mental subjugation had been identified. Discussions and meetings were being held at all levels of society, across racial and social boundaries. With his charming, intelligent, and light-skinned wife as ambassador, my father was introduced to open-minded people in all walks of life: radical intellectuals, daring businessmen, leaders seeking social justice. All were ready to listen to Howell's proposals and were trying to create links with his community in a new, more democratic society. Dada became friends with the leaders of the largest immigrant groups, including Albert Chang, a figurehead in the Chinese community; Baba Tewari, chief of the Indian settlement in West Kingston; and Edward Hanna, a young Syrian entrepreneur who was to become one of the most successful businessmen in Jamaica.

Dada was bursting with ideas and energy and he and my mother planned a six-month trip overseas. The full details of the trip were published in the *Gleaner* on June 5, 1939. The president of the Ethiopian Salvation Society and his wife/secretary were to leave in July for New York City, where they would attend the organization's international convention, and afterward embark to London. In the British capital, my father would pay a visit to George Padmore of the

International African Service Bureau, and to Ladipo Solanke, leader of the West African Students Union. They would then proceed to the west coast of Africa to meet with African political leaders and prepare for a grand jubilee in Jamaica in August 1940; several dignitaries from Africa would be invited.

During this period, Dada also made a new enemy: the trade unions. Out of the 1938 rebellion arose a new class of politicians who saw him as a rival. The colonial establishment hated my father, and chief among them was Alexander Bustamante, president of the Bustamante Industrial Trade Union (BITU), who later became chief minister of Jamaica, and eventually prime minister. Bustamante was one of the most powerful men in the nation and hated my father's influence over the workers Bustamante sought to control and put to work on plantations.

Dada knew the terrible things that went on in the cane fields: slave-labor conditions, short pay . . . and he would encourage people to be self-sufficient, telling them, "Do not work for them, work for *yourself*! If we get together, a lot of us, and pool our resources, we can buy things in quantity, we can build our houses together." The colonial establishment knew that if people started working for themselves, there would be less for the masters. Dada was interfering with the powers that be.

In order to drive Dada out of St. Thomas, several attacks on his group were carried out by the authorities. June 25, 1939, was an exceptionally bloody day in the history of my father and his Rasta followers. A group of thugs stoned and attacked one of his meetings with clubs and machetes; several people sustained serious injuries and three were blinded in one eye.

On July 6, 1939, Bustamante wrote a letter to the colonial secretary "strongly suggesting" that the inspector of police for St. Thomas arrest my father and put him back in a psychiatric hospital. He wrote: "Howell is the greatest danger that exists in this country today." A few days later, on the premises of a woman named Mrs. Samms in Port Morant, another one of my father's meetings was attacked by a group of thugs from the union.

Around this time, the colonial secretary was also getting disturbing reports from London: Leonard Howell was being sent literature by the International African Service Bureau, a Pan-African and Black Marxist organization led by Trinidadian journalist George Padmore, C.L.R. James, Amy Asherwood Garvey, and Jomo Kenyatta.

It was time the Rastas found a place of their own. That would be the only way to put an end to the unjust treatment they were receiving from every direction: the British colonial government, the local authorities, the police, the unions, and even sectors of the Jamaican public.

As it happens, the 1939 trip overseas never took place, for several reasons. First, my mother discovered that she was pregnant with her first child, my older brother Monty. My parents were also in the final negotiations for the purchase of an old estate in the parish of St. Catherine, an area where they and their followers might be safe. The name of the estate was "Pinnacle." On April 25, 1939, the land title was transferred to Albert Chang, who had become a very good friend of my mother's. The plan was for Chang to then sell the property to the Ethiopian Salvation Society. My mother, twenty-seven and pregnant, was eager to move to Pinnacle as soon as her child was born. She decided to sell all her jewelry, including a beloved set of pearl earrings and matching necklace, to pay Chang the first installment of the purchase: £1,200. My parents paid eight hundred pounds in cash as a down payment; the balance of four hundred would be paid later. My father had opened a second bakery, and business was going well, producing a steady income for the family.

On December 3, 1939, Tenneth gave birth to her first son. My brother Montinol "Monty" Anthony Howell was born at 2 Ivy Green Crescent, St. Andrew. Shortly after his birth, the family officially relocated to Pinnacle. Our records show that 1,100 members moved there in 1940. People came from different parishes; the largest group was from St. Thomas, the second largest from Clarendon, followed by Kingston and others.

The conditions for the first settlers were rough. They did not have shelter; they did not have anything. They had to build their own houses. Every day, groups of men would cut wood and haul it to the area where they planned to establish the village of "East Avenue"; others would set the foundations or build temporary shelters so that people could camp; still others cleared land and started planting crops. The people who could not handle the hardships left—but most stayed.

Under the leadership of my father, the community experienced tremendous growth for all sixteen years of its existence.

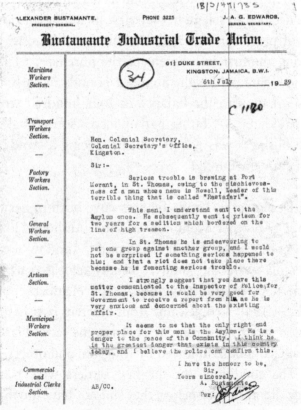

Letter from Alexander Bustamante to the colonial secretary, July 6, 1939: "This terrible thing that is called 'Rastafari'" (Jamaican Archives, Spanish Town).

PART II

PINNACLE

Aerial photo of East Avenue.

A STRATEGIC LOCATION

Pinnacle was a very big estate. As a kid, I was told that it was some two thousand acres of hills and valleys, cliffs and caves, a maze of wilderness with narrow trails. We made use of most of the land by cultivating hundreds of fields for our cash crops and personal consumption. A large, dilapidated house was still standing at the top of a steep hill, overlooking the plain and the sea. This was what we called the "big house" or "great house," and the view from it was incredible. You could see 360 degrees to distant parts of the island, from the St. Ann parish down to Kingston, Port Royal, and the Palisadoes (now Norman Manley) Airport.

Pinnacle was located in a strategic spot: any person in command of the island—the governor or a general—would want to be stationed there. You could see every ship coming into Kingston Harbour, every plane taking off or landing, any vehicle approaching from miles away. I can understand why the Spaniards built this great big house at Pinnacle in the first place.

Without a doubt, it was a lookout post. And it became a lookout for us too; there could never be a surprise attack (or so we thought). And when we shouted from up there, the sound would travel for miles.

My family lived in what was left of that big old house on top of the hill, the highest point in the surrounding area. The architecture of the main building was Spanish, with five beautiful brick arches, all in a terrible state of disrepair. Beside it was a smaller cottage, also in a shambles. My father rebuilt both structures, but the strong winds would always tear the roof off the big house as soon as he could repair it, so he decided to settle the family in the cottage. It's a total ruin now, though when we first arrived, the walls and part of the roof were still standing. There was quite a lot of woodwork still in place. I do not remember the condition of the front parts facing Spanish Town, but in back there were good rooms, usable living space.

We had running water inside the great house as well as the cottage. Both came from rainwater collected on the roofs and fed into catchments through separate gutter systems. Water from the big house was caught in a big tank made of cement and stone and distributed through pipes and taps. You could wash dishes, flush the toilet, water the plants and animals, and do other cleaning, but since those taps had been there for quite some time and were made of lead, the tank water was not fit for drinking unless you boiled it first. At some stage, the house had probably suffered a major fire—maybe more than one, because when you walked around, you could find pieces of lead the size of my hand. Water for drinking and food preparation came from four metal hundred-gallon tanks that were replenished from the cottage gutter system and from what people would haul up and fill.

The largest settlement of followers was below the great house. Pinnacle was situated on the edge of the Jamaican highlands; it was very windy up there, and if you built a structure on a flat area, it would be blown down in no time. So when the people first came, they were looking for a spot protected on all sides from the strong winds. They found a small clearing between the hills, and over time, little by little, they built hundreds of houses. They were constructed in a style common among poor Jamaicans—dirt floor, thatch roof, wattle and daub walls (tree branches covered with mud)—but the homes were theirs and they took pride in them. We called the village "East Avenue." Even today there's still an *East Avenue* sign, but the land has been bulldozed and it now looks very different.

When the people first started moving in, they built an extra-large kitchen area in East Avenue where food was cooked for everybody in huge pots. It was flanked by three or four large porches which served as dining rooms and meeting halls. The cooking and baking supplies were stored in a pantry. In the first two years, food was free for all settlers. To feed 1,100 people, my father had to purchase cornmeal, corn, and flour from the Chinese wholesale merchants in Kingston.

But after two years of struggle and hard work, everybody would have their own kitchen and cook their own produce.

I do not remember seeing people eating in the mess hall, because that phase ended while I was a baby. Yet those massive pots were still there, and they reminded me of the pots I saw in comic strips in the *Daily Gleaner*. At that time, the Phantom and Tarzan were the most popular superheroes. In these cartoons, huge pots like ours were used by Black African cannibals to cook white people, but without fail, the white superhero would appear and rescue the white damsel in distress in the nick of time.

One pot had a crack in it and could not be used anymore, so my brother and I tried to smash it with big stones—we were devils. But it was cast iron, probably from one of the sugar mills, so it didn't break, and Monty seriously injured his knee while trying to destroy it.

My father designed a brick oven and other supporting buildings for a bakery near our home. We dug a well and the water was supposed to be pumped up to the cottage, and it was for some time, but it wasn't consistent, so we mainly relied on the four metal drums instead. About a mile away from the houses, set in a valley, we built a humongous tank of concrete and stone that was fed by rainwater catchments and used exclusively for the animals.

There were only two entrances to Pinnacle. The main

gate was off Sligoville Road, in the area we called "Camp" or "Down Camp." This was where 80–90 percent of all business transactions took place. The other entrance was off what is now called Emperor Haile Selassie Highway, miles away on the other end of the property.

A lot of people, including some famous Rastas, have claimed that they visited Pinnacle. But the question is *where* in Pinnacle did they go? Visitors rarely entered unannounced into East Avenue because all strangers had to be escorted there. Family members, however, could enter at their own will. I've heard rumors that Mortimer Planno visited, but I actually remember when Count Ossie did.

Photograph from a Jamaican police magazine, 1955.

THE NEIGHBORHOOD

||||||||||||||||||||||||||||||||||||||||||||||||||||||||||||||||||||||||||||||||||||||||||||||||||||

When my parents first arrived at Pinnacle, the people from the valley were hostile to us. Rasta was being introduced to Kingston in the 1940s by Pinnacle people who went to Coronation Market (the biggest outdoor market in Jamaica at that time) to sell their goods. Opposite Coronation Market, on the other side of Darling Street, there was a community called Back-o-Wall where a lot of young men lived in shacks. They were not employed; they eked out a living moving goods to and from the market and delivering them throughout Kingston on their homemade handcarts. They were unkempt and they did not shave or cut their hair, so people called them "beardmen"; that look existed long before my father started Rasta. These young beardmen were among the first to pick up the Rasta culture and ideology. But as we used to say, not all Rastas were beardmen, and not all beardmen were Rastas.

Pinnacle people—Howellites, Rastas, and beardmen—had to walk in groups because they could be assaulted. In those days, we had no transportation; to go to Kingston or Spanish Town, you had to walk several miles to a place called Crossing which was on the main thoroughfare, then pass through Thompson Pen, Waterloo, and other villages where the inhabitants were extremely unfriendly.

In 1941, we still had problems with our neighbors. The Pinnacle estate had been abandoned for decades and the local people had come to think of it as theirs to plant, pick fruit, gather bat manure, and make coal. In those first years, we sold our own charcoal and the income helped with our food situation, but it also created a conflict with some of our neighbors who had been using our land to do the same.

One day in December 1941, some men came over to steal the coal we had made. There was a verbal confrontation, and then a big fight broke out. A group of Pinnacle men beat the intruders, who in turn went to the nearest police station and reported that Rastas were stealing from them and attacking them. Since my father was the head of the community, the police considered him responsible and came to arrest him. They didn't even try to gather facts or investigate the area where the fight had taken place. My father didn't have anything to do with this fight, but the police claimed that he had given the orders. Around a hundred men were arrested, including Dada. In its 1960 "Report on the Rastafari Movement in Kingston," the University of the West Indies stated that my father had called for the raid on a neighbor's farm and then ordered that one of the offenders receive ninety-one lashes. Those false allegations, like so many others, were subsequently repeated elsewhere, including in several books.

Dada was not a cruel man. He was a peacemaker who believed in nonviolent solutions. Furthermore, he would never have allowed his followers to trespass on other people's property. *We* were the ones who got raided!

My father declared his innocence, but a magistrate in Spanish Town found him guilty and sentenced him to two years of hard labor. Everybody living at Pinnacle knew that Dada was targeted simply because he was the leader of the compound. The authorities thought they had found an opportunity to drive my father and his followers off the land—but it didn't work. Dada went to prison, but Pinnacle held on.

Over the years, people became friendlier. Locals began to speak well of us as we gained their respect and even love. People who lived in the surrounding villages initially had better living conditions than Rastas at Pinnacle, but after those first two years our community was prospering, and the people inside no longer struggled as much as the people outside. There was camaraderie at Pinnacle and even social events. Before long, Pinnacle had developed a strong sense of community—everybody was getting along and nobody was hungry . . . people felt secure.

* * *

I was born at Pinnacle on January 28, 1942, while my father was away serving his two-year prison sentence. I did not see him very often during my infancy. He was arrested again in 1944, a few months after his release, this time for allegedly murdering my mother.

AN UNSUNG HERO

Among those who questioned British rule or bemoaned the status quo, Dada was one of the few who was forging a new path. He had been notorious throughout the country since the 1930s, and now with Pinnacle, and people behind him, Dada was becoming too powerful for the colonial establishment. Under British rule, anyone considered to be in opposition to their views had to be stopped, with or without any pretext. It was not only my father, it was *anyone* who voiced their opinion. Many were sent to prison or otherwise silenced.

I do not have any memory of my mother—I was quite young when she died. But I remember that many people in the community idolized her. To them, she was like a saint, but to my father and the movement, she was so much more.

When everyone first arrived at Pinnacle and my parents were the ones providing the food, my mother looked after all the children. In the evenings, she would go around and make sure that every kid had

SATURDAY, JULY 19, 1941.   JAMAICA TIMES

SHE WAS LEFT —BEHIND—

Mrs. Howell, the former Miss Bent of St. Elizabeth.

"HE WAS A GOOD HUSBAND"

SAYS WIFE OF RAS TAFARIAN CHIEF

LAIR OF LOST MEN IS SILENT NOW

MRS. HOWELL BELIEVES ONLY IN ONE MAN

I WAS AMONG THE RAS TAFARIANS after Howell had fled, not so much as a news man seeking a good story but rather in the role of a Samaritan, when a Police Officer indicated a fair and frail woman sitting near the door of the deposed Chieftain's home, "That's Howell's wife over there," he said, "she has also left her behind."

Her head was drooped in sorrow. Her courage had given way to despair. She did not stir as I approached. Since morning she had become used to strange and heavy footsteps. Those of hostile civilians. Those of the law. At her skirts a little boy tugged. Howell's and hers.

She raised her head slowly as if hoping that the scene had changed—a seemingly-un-ending nightmare of men moving about swinging sticks, batons, machetes.

Yet her thoughts were not of herself, not of her humiliation before the eyes of the serfs who once comprised her "Kingdom", but of—the man whom they believed was their King. The man she still loved—her husband. And yet, she accepted her plight. For she believes in fate; in God. Perhaps she could have been a school teacher, and he a doctor. But as Miss Bent, the promising "young miss" of the small St. Elizabeth district, she had deserted the schoolroom; he had tossed aside his medical books. Subsequent developments were guided by a hand which could not be detained.

'A STERN WOMAN'

When her eyes finally came to rest on me, they held a blank stare; were red and a bit swollen—due to crying no doubt. But bereft of their sadness, her features were those of a stern woman. Perhaps not a cruel one, but a woman who could issue orders to many a man and see them carried through.

She said nothing until I spoke, and even then responded to my query with great reluctancy.

"Where's Howell?", I bluntly asked. But she had been similarly interrogated so many times before, that she didn't worry to question authority, she just gave me the stereotype line: "I don't know".

I believed her. Not that I just took her word for it but you would too, if you heard the way she said it, looking far into the distance as if into a world beyond her gaze she muttered softly, I believe only in one man, I have faith in Him; so long as he stands by me I shall have no fear".

"Who's that?" I asked, to make sure if it was Howell. "The Lord God Almighty" she said.

I meant to ask her how come that be when the Ras Tafari professed faith only in Ras Tafari. But I didn't desire to further embarrass her.

CURIOUS CIVILIANS

"Couldn't you ask the police to get some of these people they were curious civilians out of the house"? she begged

When they came out—that is, most of them—we went in

The trek up to Pinnacle is not so easy. I was thirsty and asked for a drink of anything.

"That is all you can have" she said, reaching over the table and handing me a bundle of guineps, "From morning
(Continued on page 3).

undergone a metamorphosis. The gate was jammed by policemen, service cars, spectators. A week before we could not enter. But now there was little hindrance.

Our first thought was of Hamilton, the gateman. A beard protruding from one of the shacks guided us to him. Perhaps the week before if he had let us in; if we had seen the Chieftain, things would have been different. But then again perhaps we would have been different when we emerged. We did not censure him; but he himself expressed our gratitude. But in the sun-paralleled scene before our eyes, Hamilton though involved soon faded into inconspicuousness.

STREAM OF EVACUEES

There was a steady stream of evacuees from the "residential section" of the Camp situate about one-and-a-half miles up. There were old men with white beards, famed women with under-nourished babies, young girls with half-exposed bodies. Their belongings were few—a mattress, an old grip, and a three-footed chair perhaps. They passed us in groups of from two to twenty, but as long as we could look they kept on coming, and all bound for nowhere.

food—this was one of her responsibilities. The conditions that existed in those first years must have been extremely difficult, but she managed to feed everyone three times a day.

Whenever Monty and I went to East Avenue, many people expressed great affection toward us when they recalled my mother and her kindness. They would rub my head and say things like, "Oh yeah, Mr. Blade"— "Blade" was my childhood nickname—"she was such a nice person. She would make sure everybody had something to eat."

Some time ago in New York City, I attended a ceremony where three women were being given awards for being important role models—two Americans and one Jamaican. One of the speakers declared that behind many outstanding enterprises there is usually a strong woman whose name is never mentioned. She asked the audience, "Can anyone think of an exception to this rule?"

Someone responded, "Rasta."

But I protested: "What about my mother? Do you not think she was a Rasta? My father could not have bought Pinnacle without Tenneth Bent-Howell, and without her, the organization would have faltered and the whole movement would have failed." She was the mother of the very first Rasta group; she was my father's intellectual equal in all his early endeavors; she served as the secretary of his Ethiopian Salvation Society; and she oversaw almost all official matters. She was right there with him, yet history has not retained her name.

* * *

My mother went missing on December 7, 1943. Her body was found several days later when someone noticed a flock of vultures ("John crows," as we call them in Jamaica) gathering not far from our home. Her body was badly decomposed.

My mother's death was the perfect way to discredit my father and bring him down. Even though Dada had left for Kingston days before my mother's disappearance and had returned two days later, he was arrested and charged with her murder.

But he had nothing to do with it, and fortunately, the charges didn't stick. After the trial, the attorney general wrote to the colonial secretary that "according to medical evidence it was impossible to specify the cause of Mrs. Howell's death and, therefore, to say that either her husband or anyone else has murdered her, I had no alternative but to enter a *nolle*." The fairness of the decision proved that justice sometimes prevails, even under colonial circumstances. But in Dada's time, it was a rare occurrence.

Although my father was acquitted of the ridiculous, trumped-up charge of murdering his wife, suspicion lingered throughout the island. He had been disliked before, and now he was despised. These suspicions soured business connections and arrangements— most importantly, the deal between Dada and Albert Chang. Chang had been a very good friend of my mother's and had helped my parents purchase Pinna-

Hon Attorney General.

63. Referred for the favour of your advice.

A.C. Chapman
for Col. Secy
31/3/44

31.3.44
381

5073/34
381/44

Hon. Colonial Secretary,

    Howell has now been released. As on
perusing the depositions I found that according to
the medical evidence it was impossible to specify
the cause of Mrs. Howell's death and, therefore,
to say that either her husband or anyone else had
murdered her, I had no alternative but to enter a
nolle.

2.   If, as I believe, Pinnacle belongs to
or is leased by Howell or his organisation,
the Government can take no steps to break up the
settlement of his followers upon that property
even though their habits and customs do not conform
to those usually adhered to in civilized communities.
The foregoing, of course, does not imply that if
evidence of breaches of the Law by Howell and his
followers is forthcoming those breaches should
not be punished, irrespective of whether they take
place on Pinnacle or elsewhere, but merely that so
long as Howell's followers observe the Law they are
entitled to continue to live unmolested in whatever
way they please.

[signature]

Attorney-General.
4.4.44.

N/f.

The attorney general's reply to the colonial secretary stating that the inhabitants of Pinnacle have the right to live as they wish and that he will respect those rights (Jamaican Archives, Spanish Town).

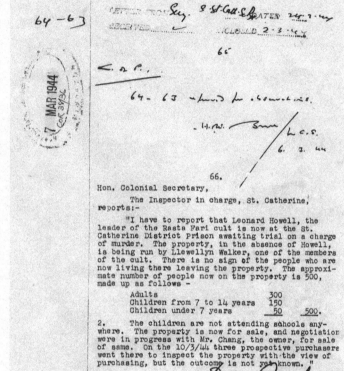

64 - 63

65

C. 2 P.

64 - 63 ~ ~~~~ ~ ~~~~~~~~.

- H. W. Bw / L. C. S.
6. 3. 44

66.

Hon. Colonial Secretary,

The Inspector in charge, St. Catherine, reports:-

"I have to report that Leonard Howell, the leader of the Rasta Fari cult is now at the St. Catherine District Prison awaiting trial on a charge of murder. The property, in the absence of Howell, is being run by Llewellyn Walker, one of the members of the cult. There is no sign of the people who are now living there leaving the property. The approximate number of people now on the property is 500, made up as follows -

Adults	300	
Children from 7 to 14 years	150	
Children under 7 years	50	500.

2.   The children are not attending schools anywhere. The property is now for sale, and negotiation were in progress with Mr. Chang, the owner, for sale of same. On the 10/3/44 three prospective purchasers went there to inspect the property with the view of purchasing, but the outcome is not yet known. "

Commissioner of Police.
25. 3. 44.

The commissioner of police to the colonial secretary, March 25, 1944: update on the conditions at Pinnacle (Jamaican Archives, Spanish Town).

cle, but everything changed after my mother's death.

In 1944, while Dada was still in jail awaiting trial, Chang decided to put Pinnacle up for sale, claiming that he still owned the land title. That caught my father by surprise. At first, neither he nor anyone else at Pinnacle took it seriously, because up until then there had never been a whisper that the two thousand–plus acres belonged to anyone *but* Leonard Howell. We thought it was just the same old propaganda, the usual harassment from the British and Jamaican authorities. There was no way they could get away with stealing our land. Or so we thought.

The October 14, 1945, issue of the *Daily Gleaner* came as a shock. It carried a full-page report with a huge headline, "Jamaica's Great Ras Tafarite Kingdom Comes to an End."

One can only wonder why Chang decided to go back on his word and reclaim the property he had sold to my parents. Chang alleged that he was never repaid the balance of four hundred pounds due on the land, and challenged my father to show the receipts—knowing full well that the police had seized most documents and books in our house over the course of numerous raids. Why would he want to take back our land and turn thousands of men, women, and children homeless? I believe he had been subjected to pressures from the power structure but had ignored them until this point.

Albert Chang was a progressive man, a railway engineer forced by circumstances to exile himself to Jamaica in 1913 and become a merchant. He was a

Jamaica's Great Ras Tafarite Kingdom Comes To An End

Daily Gleaner, October 14, 1945.

Albert Chang

Edward Rasheed Hanna

humanist, a founding member of the People's National Party (PNP), and a leader in the Chinese community of Jamaica. He was open to interracial relations and cooperation with local people—hence, probably, his initial positive attitude toward my father's experiment. So it was likely my mother's death and all the rumors spreading about my father and his followers in "good and polite" society that convinced the aging businessman to put an end to a situation that he didn't want his children to inherit.

Albert Chang died in March 1946, before my father was exonerated in the murder case. Chang's will stated that if he did not find a buyer, ownership of Pinnacle would be transferred to the Boy Scouts Association, which he had been sponsoring. The administrator general for Jamaica was registered as executor of Chang's estate, and in February 1947 the title of Pinnacle was transferred to Reginald Norman Fletcher, Edward Rasheed Hanna, and Henry Douglas Tucker, "pursuant to the will of Albert Chang."

The legal process of dispossession was complete—though it would be many years before any of us, including Dada, learned about the fraudulent changes made to the registration of Pinnacle ownership, depriving us of all our rights. But curiously enough, the new owners did not interfere with us, and the time of Chang's death coincided with the beginning of a period of relative peace and rapid development for the Pinnacle community.

A NEW ERA: 1946–1954

||||||||||||||||||||||||||||||||||||||||||||||||||||||||||||||||||||||||||||||||||||||

S ome people could not take the pressure of bush living and decided to leave, though others arrived. Yet from about 1943 onward, very few new people came to Pinnacle to live permanently. Because the community was tight—one for all and all for one—most of the land was occupied and everyone knew everyone else. It was a feeling of *We against them! We are Pinnacle people!* Dada's followers belonged to something which they did not always fully understand, but the culture made them feel better off than those outside of Pinnacle.

Pinnacle people were just as poor as anyone else, though now they had a communal value system: they worked, lived, and shared in community with one another. I remember Sister Gertrude Campbell (my father's final lieutenant) and the joyous, spirited feeling you got from her sometimes—that was the attitude and vibration at Pinnacle. It was like a high that stimulated you into behaving kindly, in a more humane way. Not like in Kingston, where it was a constant rat race, one side fighting the other . . . Life for poor people was a lot harder there.

People in Pinnacle were relaxed, there was unity and togetherness. Even if they were still poor, there was a richness of the mind. At Pinnacle, we were not primarily focused on religion. So when people said they were Christians or Bobo Shantis or Nyabing-his, it did not matter to us. "What matters," Dada preached, "is not depending on anyone else, and moving forward together. Instead of making war, make peace! Work beside your brother and sister, cultivate unity, and you can develop the strength to achieve what you think is right. The system only serves one master. When you work for a master, you are making someone *else's* life better."

We were almost like a country within a country, and this was disturbing to the government.

And yet, the winds had started to change for Pinnacle. Some voices in society had begun condemning the harassment to which our family and our people were subjected. In the 1944 letter in which the attorney general had declared a *"nolle,"* the AG went on to advise the colonial secretary:

> *If, as I believe, Pinnacle belongs to or is leased by Howell or his organization, the Government can take no steps to break up the settlement of his followers upon that property even though their habits and customs do not conform to those usually adhered to in civilized communities.*

This letter clearly shows that the attorney general was resisting pressures from other forces. He had to remind them that there were still laws in the British Empire.

My father also benefited in other ways from the new political situation. 1944 was the year when adult suffrage was finally implemented. Now that poor people could vote, they had to be taken into consideration. My father received letters from politicians asking him to influence his people for their vote. During general elections, each party would send a delegation up to Pinnacle to try to garner his support. PNP was trying to get him, JLP (Jamaica Labour Party) was trying to get him, yet he never endorsed either. He favored PNP—that was his private opinion since their platform was closer to his social outlook—but he never made a statement about this nor told anyone who to vote for.

A lot of people living at Pinnacle didn't vote, but if they had a desire to do so, they were free to support whichever candidate they liked. The politicians needed votes, so they tried all kinds of tactics to get us involved. Once, they came and asked the people, "What can we do for you?"

Someone said, "Can you bring water up to Pinnacle?"

The man answered that it was too far, so the people decided not to give them their votes. And that was that.

WATER

||||||||||||||||||||||||||||||||||||||||||||||||||||||||||||||||||||||||||||||||||||

Water was probably the biggest difficulty at Pinnacle, and there were several ways to deal with it. Everyone would have a catchment system: bamboo trees split in half lengthwise and fixed to the side of a roof, which would trap rainwater in a tank or wooden barrel. Gutter systems can be very effective, but sometimes in Jamaica when it doesn't rain for long periods, you can run out of water.

In the early days, the nearest public standpipe was far away. During the dry season, you had to go to the Caymanas Estate, which was miles away from Pinnacle. Then, in 1950, the government brought a standpipe to Waterloo, which was only three miles away. Although not as close as we would have liked, it was a big improvement. We would load kerosene cans on each side of our donkeys' backs and a party of young boys and girls would take them to the Waterloo standpipe and fill the cans. We also had several dray carts driven by donkeys to take our goods to Kingston. But the dray cart transport systems were a real danger at night, especially with motorcycles. They only had one dim little kerosene lantern you wouldn't see until you were right upon them. Despite that, the carts were a great help with the water situation.

Now and then some people brought water up the steep, rocky dirt track on the southeast corner of the property, which was a shorter distance but almost impossible to climb. Only the fittest among us could go up that way, like this guy Tilbert Black, or Gerald "Bunny" Downer. I can still see them climbing the rocks with those cans of water on their heads . . . That was a feat!

Another source of water were the hundreds of water holes all over the property. Whenever it rained, the water would settle inside the honeycomb rocks that covered most of Pinnacle; vegetation would grow over them, so they remained cool and held water all year long. When we were thirsty at Down Camp, we just went looking for a water hole. When it was dry everywhere else, you could get the sweetest drink from those little crevices in the ground. But to find them, you had to know where to look.

Sometimes during a dry spell, you would have to go down to the Rio Cobre river. It was hard coming up into East Avenue from that side, because you had to walk up a very steep trail. Occasionally kids would go down that way and bring back a can of water for us; it was probably Edgard Reid, one of my father's lieutenants, who told them to do so. But in our house at the top of the hill, we had multiple ways of getting water, including a big tank and the four hundred-gallon metal drums.

A mysterious thing happened during the last few years of Pinnacle's existence: a pond began to form in East Avenue.

At first the water settled naturally at the lowest point when it rained, then in winter it would dry out. We brought the cattle there to drink; horses and cows would trample the surroundings and mud would fill the crevices. After some particularly heavy rainfalls, we discovered that we had a good-sized pond all year round. We could not drink the water but we could swim in it. For fun, we'd bring bamboo up from the river and make rafts to float around on, and after a time bamboo started growing there too. There was oil nut (from which castor oil is made) all around the edges.

In the early days of the year-round pond, the water was murky, and when it finally settled, insects started to proliferate. I decided that if animals could live in there, fish could too, so I caught several types of fish from the river. The first I brought in was a bottom fish we called "mogo mogo," a scavenger. Then I put in mullets and sandfish. Sandfish have a shovel mouth which they use to bury themselves. To catch them you had to "mash fish," which meant you walked slowly in the water, twisting your foot in the sand with every step. When you stepped on a fish, you would feel it wiggling and you could capture it. Some of the other kids helped me bring in the fish, but I was the main instigator.

That pond was also a minor disaster at times, because when it rained hard, the people in the nearest row of houses would be flooded out. The water would seep in, and people had to find accommodations elsewhere.

PINNACLE PRODUCTIONS

||||||||||||||||||||||||||||||||||||||||||||||||||||||||||||||||||||||||||||||

F arming was the main way we made a living. There was more land in Pinnacle than people could possibly cultivate, and we grew all types of produce.

We ate a lot of ground food: yams, potatoes, and cassavas. We did not plant very much rice—we had to bring that in from the outside—but we had plantains, sweet potatoes, corn, gungu peas, red peas, and various other types of peas and beans.

When times were hard, we always had fruit, and something or another was always in season. You name the fruit, we had it in abundance. I think the reason there were so many fruit trees at Pinnacle was because of the bats. There were two caves where thousands of them lived. They went off for miles around and ate all kinds of fruit, and on their flights back they deposited their droppings, and then berries and seeds would grow. There was a mango area, a naseberry area, a sweetsop area, a pear (avocado) area . . . Bat droppings are one of the best organic manures, and we mined the caves for it. We were the first to commercialize it in Jamaica, and it provided a good income for Pinnacle people; we had literally tons of the stuff that had just been lying there for hundreds of years.

I did not take part in the planting—I worked with the animals. I was the trainer, so when a new mule had to be broken in, I was the one to "buck" it. I could ride anything—except Big Sid.

When I was a youth, a circus came to Jamaica and they had a monster bull named Big Sid. One hundred percent sure that no one could ride this thing, they offered a cash prize of a thousand pounds to anyone who could stay on for ten seconds. Although I was only eleven or twelve years old, I was big and tall, so no one questioned my age and they let me enter the contest. Running under the bull's belly and up to its massive back, there was a rope handle, but when I sat on the back of this beast, I suddenly realized how big and wide it was. My legs were stretched so far apart that I couldn't get a grip and couldn't keep my balance. I didn't get the thousand pounds. I don't think anyone won the prize money.

On the property, I rode horses, mules, and donkeys with my friends: Lester Powell, Hedley Black, Tut and Merryman Barrett, Freddyman Gylmore, Lowie Campbell, Baba Shaw, Roy Black, Lenny, Percy, Bunny . . . We would catch whatever animal we wanted, then we'd ride to the river or to Thompson Pen. Sometimes we would have races. I was the one who decided who should ride what. I used to ride a huge brown mule named Baby; no one else would ride her. Mules and donkeys were our local transportation. We didn't use them to plow fields, though—most of the land was not leveled. We had mules to pull the carts. Horses were too finicky and were likely to break a leg—unlike a donkey, the most sure-footed animal (and the favorite transportation of Jesus Christ, they say).

I was given a very special dog by an old couple and I named him Lion because of his looks. The lion occupied a high place in my father's vision. He sometimes included it in his Rasta flag. The lion was a symbol of Africa: it represented courage, integrity, and sovereignty. This dog could count to ten. If you told him a number, he would pat, *One, two, three . . .* with his paw. He was also a great herder. Whenever we wanted to catch a certain goat, we had Lion smell its droppings and off he would go, picking and cutting that goat away from the herd and driving it to us. He was quite an incredible dog; I don't know who trained him. Maybe the name carries with it an elevated intelligence, because my grandson, Lion—named in homage to my father—also has a very high IQ.

Mr. Campbell was the chief baker, and husband to Sister Gertrude Campbell. They were parents to one of the best drum players I've ever heard and who still plays to this day—Louie Campbell. Baking had been Mr. Campbell's profession before he came to Pinnacle. Now he oversaw the entire operation: he baked buns, bullas, and beef patties; we had two main types of bread, white hard dough and corn bread, and a smaller one with butter in it. My father knew something about baking since he had been a cook on ships during the war and had run successful bakeries, but Mr. Campbell was the chef. I think a few shops in Waterloo and Three Miles bought small quantities from our bakery, but the production was basically for Pinnacle people. There were different places in East Avenue to which bread was delivered early in the morning so people could have fresh bread and milk for breakfast.

No one in Pinnacle had livestock, except my father. He bought the cows because he needed milk for his bakeries and for the community. The cows were not for eating, although occasionally that did happen. Whenever they slaughtered one, they would distribute the meat to whoever wanted beef. I think people paid a small amount of money, something like two pence a pound, for the men who looked after the cows. They were the ones who ran the show.

Before dawn, the men in charge would milk the cows, then bring the milk back to East Avenue where it was scalded and pasteurized. They did not use a machine, they boiled it in large zinc pans, the kind the British used to stock petrol. Once boiled, the fat would then be skimmed off. All that had to take place by six or seven a.m., before people got up and wanted their milk. We also made butter, cheese (though not very successfully), and sometimes even ice cream, which was a novelty for me.

Cows had ticks that the birds would pick off, leaving small wounds that would become infected and could turn into nasty lesions with large worms. We had to disinfect the cattle once or twice a year, and we used a simple system for that: we dug a trench in the ground, with the deepest part in the middle, and we filled it with water and disinfectant (we used DDT powder, which was later banned by the US Environmental Protection Agency), then we made the animals walk through the mixture, one by one, so that it covered their entire bodies.

This type of activity required a lot of human labor, so when we needed to do it, my father would ask for volunteers. The men would be there the next morning to set about their work, while Monty and I got in the way as usual.

When we started raising goats, we kept them in a pen. Soon there were too many and they broke out, so we decided to let them run loose. They always stayed together, moving all over the land in a herd.

A horse, mule, or donkey would sometimes wander off the property. Whenever this happened, our neighbor and wealthy landowner, Joseph Watt, would alert the animal pound, who would immediately take the animal away. We would have to pay a fine to get it back. Eventually, some of the men built fences and other barriers at strategic points around the perimeter of our property. I don't know how they accomplished that feat, but it took some careful engineering, and we finally managed to keep all the livestock on Pinnacle land.

In the final years at Pinnacle, we had many hundreds of goats, possibly a thousand or more. Before we moved out, Monty and I caught and sold some of them, though the majority were left behind; the people could not take them along. After we left, when people in the area wanted to have a feast, they would simply catch some goats and slaughter them. Many were still there when I left Jamaica in 1969. I wouldn't be surprised if some of them or their offspring remain in the untamed parts of the property today.

People used to cook with charcoal, so we made our own. There were trees in abundance on the property and we were skilled at burning charcoal. That is something I can still do today. You cut the wood and stack it in such a way that the pieces support each other and don't cave in, packing the little ones around the big ones, but there should always be a passage for air—so you put a pole in the ground and pack all the wood around it. You make a big kiln, cover it with leaves, then with dirt, and finally you pull the pole out and start the fire inside. It burns slowly for three or four days, and then you can open it and collect the coal.

When we got our own vehicle, Monty and I started a grocery shop. We were still very young at the time; I was eleven and Monty was thirteen. Other people had their little shops, mostly in East Avenue, but ours was situated at Camp, close to the front gate. Camp was as far as an outside person could come into Pinnacle unaccompanied. It was basically the transit point; all goods would enter or be stored there until they were shipped to Kingston. A lot of activities took place at Camp; people were always milling about. There were different clusters of houses at different times; our shop was the smallest building. We sold flour and cornmeal, cheese, sugar, salt fish, bar soap to wash clothes, bath soap, and soft drinks. We would buy our supplies in Kingston from Chinese merchants on Barry Street, the early importers and wholesalers of dry goods. We ran the shop for several years.

At Camp, there was also a shoe factory. "Power shoes" made at Pinnacle were popular items in Jamaica in those days. The shoemakers would go to Kingston and buy old car tires; they would cut out the bottom to make the soles and used the inner tubes for the strips; they had rubber on the front and back, so your feet were well protected. Sometimes different materials were used for the top. We made a female model, a sort of slipper, and sometimes we would make a fancy pair, but most were for men who worked outdoors in the fields, in the mud, especially farmers. Those shoes were very strong, very durable; there was no other footwear like them. They were not very attractive, but they served their purpose. I quickly caught on to how they were crafted and I made several pairs as gifts for my girlfriends. Power shoes were so popular that we could sell more than we could make. People from all parts of the country bought them. "Creps" (tennis shoes) had not yet arrived in Jamaica and poor people mainly walked barefoot. I myself walked without shoes for a long time. I had shoes, of course, but living at Pinnacle, I wanted my feet to toughen up like everyone else, and after a while the soles of my feet got so thick that I could run on freshly cut stone.

And there was a lot of that at Pinnacle too—people used to sell cut stone, it was another source of income. They would extract large rocks from the mountainside and break them into smaller pieces. Many people had their own piles, and building companies would come to buy stones from them. The government's public works department was our largest customer. They were acknowledging the fact that we were there, and productive. We had good relationships with the public works department on that level.

ADMINISTRATION

O n November 23, 1940, the *Gleaner* printed the following headline: "Howell, an Absolute Monarch in Socialist Colony." This curious description of my father had some truth to it. Dada was authoritative—that's just who he was. There were endless meetings, but Dada always had the last word. He was the one who delegated duties to people or removed them when they messed up. In fact, everything at Pinnacle was technically his, although it was run on a communal basis. Once he made his decision, any dispute was over. "Counselor says we should not plant . . ." "Counselor says we must link a road to so-and-so . . ."

Different committees oversaw different matters. There was one that showed people when and where to start planting and what seeds to use. Someone might hear about a better type of corn, and new seeds would be distributed. If someone heard about a disease that was spreading, the herbal remedy would be shared. Anything related to farming, milking, cow diseases, or building roads was decided by committees, but over-all, Dada had the final say. He was the one with the vision, he was the one who was financing it, and when the colonial powers decided to strike, he was the one who got sent to prison.

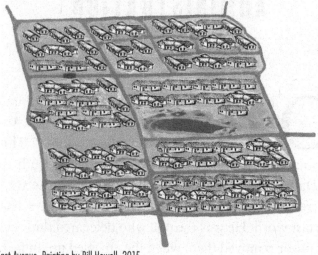

East Avenue. Painting by Bill Howell, 2015.

* * *

The bakeries in Kingston were still doing exception-ally well. We had a newspaper in which we sold ad-vertising space, and some money was trickling in from Pinnacle products too. People who lived there con-tributed a small amount, which was meant to pay for burial expenses when someone died on the compound. The people would give what they could, sometimes more, sometimes less. Nobody was punished for not paying. Besides, nobody was keeping books anyway. And if Dada had any financial records, they would have been seized in the various raids and shakedowns.

People showed their gratitude by planting something for Dada. They would choose a small plot of land and say, "This is Counselor's field." They would work it among themselves, cut the bushes down, sow the seeds, harvest the produce, and sell it in the market, then give my father the proceeds. In the 1950s, some people decided to pool together and plant a crop of ganja for Dada: "That the Counselor's own!" They gave him the money they got from that field; it was their contribution.

Everything was done on trust. There were no enforcers of any kind. We had no need for a security system, a police force, or the government. The 1960 report by the University of the West Indies says that Dada had guards and guard dogs, but that is not true—we never had guards. In the beginning there was the lookout, but we never had a security force as such.

Our people didn't have weapons; we were totally nonviolent. At the time of the 1954 raid, the *Daily Gleaner* wrote that a dreadlocked guard had been arrested with a gun. They published a photo, suggesting that this guy was a Rasta and one of us, but we didn't know him. In those days, dreadlocks were not an exclusive feature of Rastas (nor have they ever been). As a child growing up at Pinnacle, I never saw anyone who looked like the dreadlock Rastas seen today. Some beardmen in Pinnacle had what we called "bushy head," but no locs, and I still have no idea who that old dreadlocked man was. Maybe he was planted there—later it was revealed that the gun he carried was police property.

In the sixteen years of its existence, Pinnacle never had a murder, serious stabbing, or any major violent incident between individuals or groups. I imagine that sometimes people stole—that happens everywhere in the world—but it was not something that you heard about.

I do remember a single incident where money disappeared from someone's home. It was not a great fortune, less than one pound, but just the idea that someone had entered a private house and taken someone else's money caused a big commotion in East Avenue. Suddenly, a young man grabbed his younger sister, pulled off his belt, and started to whip her. It was the first time I had seen such violence. The girl had been staying in Kingston for some time, but her parents had found out that she was keeping bad company, so they had sent her back to her brother in Pinnacle. I don't know how he knew or guessed that she was the thief, but she cried, "Yes, yes, I'll give it back," and she ran for the money and apologized to the family. I don't believe in hitting people as punishment, yet I imagine the brother was so overwhelmed with shame that he took it upon himself to do what he thought was right.

There were no police involved. You do not need authority figures to tell you what to do and what not to do. Rasta is self-enlightenment, self-awareness.

"Come alive and be a forward-thinking person."

"Every action creates a reaction, so think about things thoroughly before you act. If *you* do it right, and *I* do it right, then everything will be all right."

To me, Pinnacle is proof that when people live on their own, without outside intrusion, they can govern themselves very well.

EDUCATION

||||||||||||||||||||||||||||||||||||||||||||||||||||||||||||||||||||||||||||||||||||||||

I n the early years, people could not send their children to school because Pinnacle kids had difficulty being admitted into the school system. The head of the St. Catherine school district wrote a letter to the governor general saying Dada and his followers were a disgrace to the entire parish, and that they should be evicted. But eventually, all the kids got registered in the Mount Moreland School and we all went there.

Dada wanted to send Monty and me to Monroe College, one of the top Jamaican high schools, but it was a boarding school, and for us that was out of the question. We could not possibly leave Pinnacle and go to a faraway boarding school with kids we didn't know. And what about the food they cooked there? Monty and I rebelled and tried everything we could to get out of it. We cried and protested and made it clear that we were simply not going. At some point, my father gave in.

We never established an official school system at Pinnacle. Not that Dada thought schooling was unimportant; we simply did not have the personnel to run it. Later, he realized that it was the first thing he should have implemented—but by then, the challenges he faced were already formidable. Among all the plans he made, this one remained unrealized.

There was some tutoring at Pinnacle. I remember how Brother Barrett's daughter, Dells, used to come around from time to time. I think she was a teacher. She was staying in Kingston or St. Thomas, but her parents were both living at Pinnacle and she tried to set up some formal structure for tutoring children there.

While most of the kids got registered at Mount Moreland, it was quite a distance away and not every parent made sure their kids attended regularly. I, for one, only went to school when I felt like it. In 1952 and '53, Dada was spending most of his time in Kingston, so if I woke up one morning and didn't want to go to school, I just didn't go. I really didn't like the food they cooked there. I knew it wasn't wise to take days off from school, because when you returned to class it was hard to catch up—so I had no one to blame but myself.

Rain was always a good justification for not going to school. When it rained in Jamaica in the forties and fifties, almost everything came to a halt. It was also a perfect excuse for laborers to skip work (your boss wouldn't be there either). Very few people owned or used umbrellas back then. We viewed them as accessories for English ladies walking in Kingston parks on sunny days—God forbid they get tanned and be mistaken for a colored person!

I used to like it when it rained. I had some of the most memorable times of my life just lying in bed listening to the rainfall. Our living quarters had a zinc roof, and I would lie there hearing all the beautiful tones and variations, the gorgeous musical composition that the rain played above me.

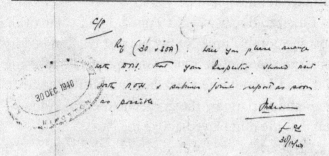

C/P

Ry (30 + 30A).   will you please arrange with D.M. that your Inspector should visit both M.O.H. & submit joint report as soon as possible.

Anderson

30/12/40

30 DEC 1940

Director of Medical Services,

                    Referred. Please issue the necessary
instructions to the M.O.H. for St. Catherine and advise me
when this has been done.

2.   I would mention that this matter is
already receiving the attention of my Department and the
Inspector in charge St. Catherine has already been in
consultation with your M.O.H with regard to the existing
sanitary conditions at Pinnacle.

                                        Commissioner of Police.
                                             2. 1. 41.

5 JAN 1941
DEPARTMENT

/22/41

Hon. Colonial Secretary,

        The Medical Officer (Health) and Inspector of Police visited the
Camp together on 11/1/41.

2.   I visited the Camp several weeks ago with the Clerk of the Board
and the Medical Officer Spanish Town. The Medical Officer (Health) was
not available.   The living conditions of the inmates whom I saw were
very unsatisfactory.   The shacks were of plain wattle and not weather-
proof; rough beds had been made of sticks with no mattresses and scanty
filthy bedding, the latrine accommodation was entirely inadequate, and
water had to be brought from some distance away.

3.   The small number of inmates whom I saw were in poor condition and
their clothing was deplorable.   Some complained to me that when food
was distributed, the stronger ones deprived the weaker.

4.   They were all armed with sticks, obviously with the intention of
scaring off visitors, and the guarded gates were opened to us only after
some pressure.   Several of the inmates were engaged on the construction
of a substantial house for their leader.

5.-

Above and right: The government's efforts to wipe out the Rastas; the assistant director of
medical services advises using the dangerous living conditions at Pinnacle as a pretext to ban the
community.

5.   I was told that the Chief Sanitary Inspector had been refused
admission a few days before, and I advised the Clerk to instruct him to
visit again and serve notices on the owner for construction of as many
latrines as were necessary, as one step in forcing him to abandon the
Camp.   I am enquiring whether this is being done.   I also suggested that
systematic inspections and inquiry should be undertaken to find and care
for cases of illness in the Camp which would help to weaken the leader's
grip on the inmates.

6.   In addition to the inadequacy of latrines, please see the Public
Health Law Section 64 (IV) in conjunction with Section 62 (2).Investi-
gation will probably reveal that the Board can serve notice on the
owner of the Camp to correct breaches of these sections.   There is
also Section 64 (VIII) (1) of which there is almost certainly a breach.
The Local Board appears to be in the excellent legal position of being
able to demand a number of expensive undertakings in the Camp with the
alternative that they may go in and do the work and charge it to the
owner; and I consider that they should shew more initiative instead of
simply "passing the buck" to Government.

                                    Jno Hall
                          Asst.Director of Medical Services.
                                16.1.41.

A.C.S,

        (30) et seq. submitted.

        2. The conditions existing at Pinnacle are a
scandal and a reproach to the Health Authorities
of the parish of St. Catherine. Steps should
be taken to disperse the misguided people of
this strange cult and the suggestions in para.
6 of (54) promise to provide effective means
for the purpose.   The owners of
the Camp where this nuisance exists are
liable under Sec. 65 Cap 71 if they do not take
steps to abate the nuisance.

        3. Refer to the C.B.H. to call on the
Parochial Health Authority (M.P.H. Bd.) to
take steps accordingly.
                                        AH
                                        10/1/41

HEALTH

||||||||||||||||||||||||||||||||||||||||||||||||||||||||||||||||||||||||||||||||||||||||||||

There is a January 1941 report from the Ministry of Health suggesting in no uncertain terms that unsatisfactory health conditions in Pinnacle could "help to weaken the leader's grip on the inmates." In the report, the inspectors reckoned that anyone dying in a Spanish Town poorhouse was from Pinnacle. But this was untrue. They were just local people, although some might have claimed they were Rastas. At Pinnacle, people's health was generally extremely good. Aside from what happened to my mother, no mysterious, violent, or accidental deaths ever took place. Only old people died there. I can remember a single time that a young person died of "natural causes," a boy in his teens—I think his name was Geddes.

We had some medically trained nurses. Kids born at Pinnacle were all home-delivered. I remember a lady called Nana who died in the mid/late 1950s—I was told that she had delivered me into this world. I can still see her face in my mind today. She was not a formally educated midwife, but she had been practicing the profession long before she joined my father's movement, and she had more experience than many doctors. She delivered almost all the kids at Pinnacle, and I cannot recall a single case of stillbirth. Every pregnant woman I knew at Pinnacle gave birth to a healthy child.

Medical doctors sometimes came to Pinnacle, but we mainly had "bush doctors" or herbalists. Chief among them was my own father, and in the last years of Pinnacle, this title of "doctor" that the people gave him would become one of the main points of contention between him and the authorities. He wasn't a doctor in the sense that he went to medical school and had a degree—but what would one call a person who knew a thousand different plants and their remedies? At times, people came to him for advice when they had a fever. Trees and bushes were his elements and he used them to conduct experiments and brew herbal mixtures. At Pinnacle, we made our own medicines and kept them in bottles; and once you knew how to use them, you had thousands of medicinal plants at your disposal.

Some bush doctors worked miracles; I can personally attest to this. They knew dozens, if not hundreds, of different plants and weeds, and how to use them to cure whatever ailment one might have. We had a plant and weed pharmacy that sold remedies: cerasee bush, fever grass, ginny grass, mint, Granny Scratch-

Scratch, ginger, velvet glove, and hundreds more. There was a lot of that going on, and people knew what they were talking about. Keep in mind that people worked with very sharp tools (knives, machetes, axes, and big wood saws), so when they got a cut, a bush doctor would make a mixture of different ingredients, and within a very short time the wound would heal.

It happened to me once, when I was eight or nine. A wild pig was running loose on the property, close to Camp, plundering fields. A group of men, women, and children got together and formed a hunting party. We were able to corner and capture the pig, and I was given the honor of killing it. So I took one of those straight machetes and I went to stab it, but my hand slid down the handle onto the sharp blade and I was severely injured. Four fingers on my left hand were cut to the bone, and the tendons of my middle and ring fingers were completely severed. Yet the Pinnacle people knew exactly what to do. They picked three different types of green bush leaves, wrapped them in a piece of cloth, and pulverized them, then squeezed the juice into the deep wounds on all four fingers. Finally, they put the residue of crushed leaves on the cuts and bandaged me up. The wounds healed in no time. But since I didn't have any surgery, the tendons were never repaired. To this day, I cannot bend the first joint on three fingers of my left hand, and the injury ruined whatever dream I had of playing the guitar.

And yes, there were diseases. The worst I can recall was an outbreak of yaws. Yaws is one of the ugliest diseases that exists, but one cure for it comes from a dogwood tree. You simply cut the bark, soak it in water, and drink a specific amount every day. It is extremely bitter and the smell is horrible. Aargh . . . but it works.

One controversial issue was vaccination. I do not remember hearing Dada say anything against it, but among the kids I grew up with, the prevalent attitude was: "These people come to inject you with something, it's no good . . . they're probably trying to kill us!" There was a big polio scare in 1950 and the Ministry of Health came to vaccinate kids in schools, and I did something stupid: I decided I wasn't going to do it.

I was in school when the truck came. The officials arrived escorted by police—which immediately made us suspicious. Some kids ran away, and since I was one of the biggest, I was sent to catch them. But I just went and disappeared myself! That was not very smart, but I had been influenced by the rumors about vaccines, and I had such little trust of the authorities. My belief was that if I got sick, someone in the community would heal me.

DIET AND DRESS CODE

|||||||||||||||||||||||||||||||||||||||||||||||||||||||||||||||||||||||||||

D ada believed in healthy eating; he was very conscious of what we put inside our bodies. Although he occasionally ate meat, his preference was vegetables and he always talked about the benefits of a vegetarian diet. He was not strict about it, but vegetables were important to him and he coaxed others to have healthier eating habits.

Another thing Dada stressed was the importance of eating eggs in the morning. He had a big container into which he would break some eggs and swallow them raw. Several times he urged me to swallow a raw egg, but I just couldn't do it. He even threatened to use his belt on me if I didn't comply, though I still couldn't follow his code; I ate pretty much what I wanted.

In our house, we used to eat a lot of ground foods: sweet potatoes, different types of yams and cassavas . . . basic Jamaican dishes. Yet there was no talk that meat was bad, and a lot of people at Pinnacle still ate it.

They even had a special way to cure meat. When

a cow was killed, the meat would be cut into little strips. You would put down a layer of salt at the bottom of a large barrel, set the strips of meat on top, and then add another layer of salt, and so on—that would preserve the meat for a very long time. Later, you could put a piece of it into your soup or pie. The meat had to be packed in a very specific way, because if it was exposed to the air or got contaminated, it would turn into one of the most putrid things you ever smelled and the whole batch would have to be thrown out.

Dada had nothing to do with the belief among some Mansions of Rasta that salt is not good. If he ever said something like that, I don't think he meant that it should apply to *everyone*. In any case, it was not a rule you had to comply with—everybody was free to choose their own diet.

Some people ate bird meat, some did not. I used to eat a lot of it. There were many kinds of birds which kids used to catch in traps or shoot with their slingshots, and we would roast them. Fish could be bought at the market or simply caught from the river. Naturally, anyone could raise their own chickens or barter with neighbors for them. Rice and peas with chicken was the staple dinner on Sunday, just like for most Jamaicans.

Pork was looked down upon. Dada used to say that it was unclean, although I saw him eat bacon more than once. But he would never eat fresh pork. Even so, other people did eat it—there were no food police looking over your shoulder to see what was in your pot. There were many vegetarians among us, but they weren't hostile to others with different customs; no one was ostracized for what they ate.

I cannot remember ever seeing my father take a drink of rum, though he liked wine. Wincarnis was his favorite, and a sure way to please him was to give him a bottle.

He chain-smoked Gold Flake and Dunhill cigarettes and also used ganja (marijuana). Occasionally someone would find a rare plant they called "makoney," a dark herb of superior quality, which they would present to him as a gift. Sometimes Dada smoked a lot, sometimes he would stop—but he did not think that ganja was a bad thing. It was a good, healing plant. People used it for all kinds of ailments, mainly glaucoma and asthma because of the medicinal properties which are only now being officially recognized.

I was aware of ganja as a kid, but until the early 1960s I did not know that people smoked it. I discovered this much later—after I had left Pinnacle. Whenever I went to Spanish Town, I'd meet these high school guys and university students, sons of the well-to-do in both the government and the opposition. Some had been abroad and were new to Rasta and just growing into it. We would hang out at a spot in front of the courthouse. I would teach them some chants and they would ask me about life at Pinnacle.

They used to smoke and chant, "Jah Rastafari, Lord of Lords, Conquering Lion of the Tribe of Judah!" I tried ganja a couple of times with them.

There was no dress code at Pinnacle. Many women would cover their hair, but that was a custom, not a rule. When you work outdoors, naturally, you want to protect your hair from the dirt. On Sundays, most women wore white kerchiefs wrapped tightly over their heads, but underneath they had natural hair, combed and plaited with coconut oil like most country people in Jamaica. In the 1950s, some of the young women took to straightening their hair, and many older ones looked down on that, but it was not considered a crime.

REASONING

IIIIIIIIIIIIIIIIIIIIIIIIIIIIIIIIIIIIIIIIIIIIIIIIIIIIIIIIIIIIIIIIIIIIIIIIIIIIIIIII

In the evenings, people would sometimes listen to the daily news being read aloud from newspapers. There were different corners in Pinnacle where readers would gather. Two were in the village of East Avenue; the main one was under a rock beside a big plum tree. Another place was in the northeast end of Pinnacle, near the second entrance to the village. I remember some of those readers being Edgar Reid, Powell, Jackson, Ward, and Marshall. People gathered around, listened, and discussed the news. Not everyone could read or write, but there was always someone who could write a letter for you. We had some very intelligent and educated people at Pinnacle despite what was insinuated in the press.

Among those who settled in Pinnacle, many had been travelers. Some were former soldiers who had fought in Europe during World War I, and a lot had been to Panama. One time some men were working on our house and I was nearby, so I overheard their conversation. A Jamaican asked a Panamanian, "How far is Panamantago from here?"

The Panamanian answered, "Poco mas arriba," meaning, "Just a little way down the road."

The Jamaican did not speak Spanish and started to get mad: "Why are you telling me to go *poke my ass in a river*?"

I have fond memories of Brother Bennett, a man in his seventies who always told stories about his time in Panama. He was a skilled carpenter tradesman, and he taught me how duppies (ghosts) count. I can still remember how to count from one to ten in this duppy language: *Minee, minana, bravo, vina, duppy, dagia, marko, chombo, charco, pong.*

My father had several lieutenants over the years: Theophilus Jackson (who had come with him from St. Thomas), Llewelyn Walker, and Edgar Reid, the last lieutenant before Gertrude Campbell took charge. Reid had spent one year in prison with my father in 1951 and was referred to as "Counselor's lieutenant." Dada was loved by his people. They saw him as almost a Christ figure and outdid each other trying to make him happy.

My father also had his share of women. Time and again, I saw women almost fighting each other just to serve him. He loved these women and they loved him. I don't know how Dada behaved with them in private, but I assume they enjoyed his company. He never had thirteen wives as the newspapers claimed, though he did have thirteen children with different women. Several ladies worked at our house, cleaning, washing, doing secretarial work. There were no men on our household staff, and I do not think any man outside the family ever slept there. Men like Reid came into the office, but the house was Dada's domain. The lion's den!

My father was not trying to separate women from men; he didn't think they were in any way different. At Pinnacle, there were no women's areas or men's areas—in all the celebrations, functions, processions, and worship, there was no gender segregation. Today, some Rastas try to separate the women, saying that females must wear scarves on their heads when they attend to prayers and so on, but my father always felt that anything a man does, a woman can do. One of his great heroes was the legendary pilot Amelia Earhart. He talked about her a lot, how brave she was. He thought that women could do things just as well as men and sometimes better—he didn't have any hangups there. I believe that if he were still alive today, he would support women's full liberation. But in those days, this was not discussed often. Black liberation was a more immediate concern—so I don't remember anything specifically said about gender equality besides, "Respect women!"

One could argue that Dada loved women too much to respect them, but he was a man of his times, reflecting some of the prevailing attitudes toward women. He could be a very seductive person; he was a Victorian gentleman and a lion all in one. I remember some women having verbal disputes over him, but there was never any big fight, scandal, or broken hearts. On the other hand, I wasn't interested in Dada's love life; those things would just fly over my head. One thing I do know: he was not a sexist; he was not one of those men who believed that women belonged only in the kitchen.

Dada's final lieutenant, Sister Gertrude Campbell, kept the community spirit going until she died in 2010. She was always with Dada, always in charge. This was just the way things were.

In addition to the lieutenants, there were "front men" who made sure things at Pinnacle were done properly. Men like Powell, Buchanan, Jackson, Ward, Black, Barrett, Marshall, Gallimore, Swaby, and Campbell. I remember Brother Powell vividly; he was very active in the early period and was one of the newspaper readers. His son Lester was a close friend of mine and Monty's.

Brother Buchanan was a stonemason and one of the men who helped to repair the big house. He was somewhat elderly and was rumored to be a Marxist. Some men often discussed philosophy, sharing their concepts, so it would not be strange if one of them began talking about Marx. In the late forties and fifties, anything controversial you said, you were labeled a Communist. The fact that there were people in Pinnacle who knew about Marxism was one of the things the British authorities feared the most.

In those days we had respect for the words *Communism* and *socialism*. Communism was romantic to us. We lived in a world cruelly divided by class. What could be better than all being equal under the law? Later, the Communist world opened, and we saw what was behind the scenes: it was not as bad as some people had been saying, but also not as good as others said . . .

But Cuba—yes! We were for Cuba 100 percent. We had supported Fidel Castro all along—even before he came to power, while he was still fighting to liberate his country. We were with him intellectually, morally, spiritually. "Empowerment of the people of Cuba!" That was one thing Dada talked about. Castro was very much respected by my father and his followers, and we were sorry when he was pushed into the arms of the Soviets and joined the Communist Bloc.

My father considered himself a socialist—but some outsiders called Pinnacle a *commune*, so my father *must* have been a Communist. Whenever the authorities came to Pinnacle, they would look for documents, invoking "suspicion of subversive activities," which gave them broad license to take anything from us. They did not say that what they found *was* subversive, they said the documents *could be*. Of course, these papers were never returned to us. How could we appeal to the colonial police to get them back? To this day, it pains me to think about how much was stolen from us.

Eventually, we created special underground

places, holes in the lime rock, where Dada could hide documents for safekeeping. Occasionally someone in the police force would warn him that a raid was going to occur on a certain date, and Dada would hide whatever he didn't want them to find. Though sometimes they came without warning.

News from Africa was highly sought after. Whenever there was a newspaper article about Africa, it was read aloud in public. I could name and identify most African countries, especially the British colonies. We did not believe that Africa was a single entity, as many Americans do. We knew it was a big place filled with different countries, tribes, and customs—and we could differentiate them.

Yet going back to Africa was not a main goal for Pinnacle people. They wanted to go to Africa eventually as visitors, bringing back presents, but not as migrants. My father never imagined that the Jamaican government was going to pay for people's passage to Africa. Dada knew there were people—such as Marcus Garvey—trying to get the government to do just that, but it was not part of Pinnacle's mission.

Sports news was followed closely, especially cricket. When the newspapers arrived, everybody wanted to know the latest score of the West Indian cricket team. We didn't have radios. In that period, it was a "superteam" made up of the best players from each of the British Caribbean islands, and for a long time they dominated cricket. Sonny Ramadhin, Alf Valentine, Frank Worrell, Everton Weekes, and Clyde Walcott were my heroes. Garry Sobers came later. George Headley was probably Jamaica's first superstar; during the twenties, thirties, and forties, he broke so many records in cricket history that everyone knew his name. It was such sweet joy for me when we beat the English team, and there was a huge celebration.

We spent a lot of our free time reading the newspapers, while elsewhere on the land men played dominoes. There was always a big game going on; sometimes a few women would play too.

IN THE LION'S DEN

IIIIIIIIIIIIIIIIIIIIIIIIIIIIIIIIIIIIIIIIIIIIIIIIIIIIIIIIIIIIIIIIIIIIIIIIIIIII

My father would spend whole weeks in Kingston. There were always things going on there that required his presence. He was a man totally dedicated to the organization. We first found out that the ownership of the property was in question in the mid-1940s, and from then on, my father and his friends spent a great deal of time meeting with and writing to lawyers. Unfortunately, the lawyers usually didn't uphold their end of the relationship; they often neglected to file key documentation, so Dada had to make new appointments. Each new appointment with a lawyer meant a new financial obligation . . . it went on and on. Some lawyers are the most corrupt people on earth—this is one lesson I learned from my father's experiences. They milked him dry.

At the age of four or five, I was not interested in the discussions of adults; I would rather be in East Avenue playing games with the other children, some of whom were our siblings. Pearl Staniger (Sister Pearl)

and Ivylyn Eunicy Williams (Sister Ivy) both lived in East Avenue and had six children with my father. Sister Pearl had Zodie, Myrtle, Jim, and Remy, and Sister Ivy had Enid and Inez. Monty and I, however, were the only two of my father's children who lived permanently in the big house on the hill.

We weren't conscious of all the tribulations Dada was going through . . . We were sad that he was so busy, because it didn't allow him to spend much time with us; but then again, when he was around, we probably didn't want him to be, because we had to do everything he said. When he was there, he was The Man and we had to obey.

When Dada was in Kingston, we were under the care of our nanny, Ethlyn Niklass. All the children called her Tatelyn, the name Monty had given her when he first learned to talk. We loved and respected her, and she was the only mother figure I ever knew. Our mother had hired her years before to help take care of Monty, then me. Her loving memory will remain with me until the day I die.

It could be very boring at home, just the two of us with Sister Ethlyn. Monty was a bit of a loner; often he would get up in the morning, have something to eat, and then head out into the woods to shoot birds. He would be gone for the whole day. So when my other brothers and sisters came to spend the summer with us, it was always a happy time. I used to beg Dada to let them come more often, especially my youngest brother Jim (who now lives in Canada with his family).

When Dada came home on weekends, he wouldn't put up with any nonsense. One day when I was six or seven, I was playing on the veranda, running around with a broomstick between my legs, pretending it was a bucking horse. I was whinnying, "Hihihihi! Hihihihi!" at the top of my lungs. Suddenly, I heard my father's deep voice booming out from his room, "BLADE"—that is what he always called me—"INSTEAD OF MAKING AN ASS OF YOURSELF, WHY DON'T YOU TRY TO ROAR LIKE A LION!" When my father shouted at me, normally I would shrink, but this outburst was so funny that I had to laugh, probably to my father's chagrin.

Children need company—you cannot have a lot of fun by yourself, and East Avenue was where all the fun was. There were dozens of kids there. The girls were there. I still remember Lovie Fairweather, my first girlfriend. Puppy love!

Dada did not like us spending all our time playing in East Avenue. Yet when he was in his office working on something, he was so focused that we could take off and he wouldn't even know. But if he realized we were gone, he would send someone to fetch us and promptly give us a spanking. Back then, corporal punishment was the law of the land; spanking or beating a kid was generally accepted, both at home and at school. Our punishment was usually a spanking with a wet towel and being confined to the bathroom for a period of time.

But as soon as Dada left for Kingston, we were free to do whatever we wanted. Tatelyn was not strict; she was very loving and didn't mind us going over to East Avenue—she probably knew she couldn't stop us anyway. Looking back, I think we took advantage of her kindness. I want to say this clearly: despite the occasional spankings, we were totally spoiled by the life we lived—so carefree, while our old man carried the weight of the world on his shoulders.

A CHILD'S PARADISE

||||||||||||||||||||||||||||||||||||||||||||||||||||||||||||||||||||||||||||||||||||||||

P innacle was a happy place for young people. Most families had two or three children, so there were a lot of kids around. Although Monty and I were relatively privileged, there was no resentment from the others. Everybody lived comfortably in their houses. I never thought of Pinnacle children as "poor." I guess some kids outside of Pinnacle might have lived a better life than us, but clothes, shoes, and money were not things we were concerned with. It was not a materialistic culture where people looked down on those who were less prosperous; we never had those kinds of thoughts. What was important was to *do* things better than your friends: run faster, swim better, climb a tall tree, or bring down a bat with a stone.

One thing that was always a big adventure for us was going to the river. Groups of us would spend the entire day down there, and you didn't need to bring lunch because all the food was already there. We caught and cooked fish and picked fresh fruit and herbs from the abundance of wild edible plants growing along the riverbank. Cashews, rose apples, guava, and the one with slime inside—star apple. Big trees, loaded with fruit! We brought the cashew nuts back home to roast at night. And sometimes, though not often, we would go over to Brownie's, a neighboring plantation, and eat our bellies full of his sweet navel oranges, grapefruit, star fruit, and guava. He didn't mind.

Another popular destination was Mango Walk. You had to cover quite a distance before arriving to "mango bush," as we called it, a part of the property where there were lots of mango trees. A big group of us young people would go there with large baskets and fill them; sometimes we used donkeys or mules to carry all the mangoes back home.

We played many different games in East Avenue. And because there were so many young people, multiple games were often played simultaneously. Ring plays or circle games were a big thing, and many of them had roots in Africa. *Manuel Road* was a game we played by sitting in a circle, facing one another with tennis ball–sized stones in each hand. When the game started, you put the two stones by the person next to you; they picked them up while handing you theirs, so that the two sets of stones were going in opposite directions. Everyone did this to the rhythm of the song, and if you were clumsy or not in sync, you could hurt your fingers. But I never saw anyone get seriously mashed up.

Go down a Manuel Road, gal and boy
Fi go bruck rock stone, gal and boy
Bruk them one by one, gal and boy
Bruk them two by two, gal and boy

If your finger mash, no cry, gal and boy
Remember a game we a play, gal and boy
Go down a Manuel Road, gal and boy
Fi go bruk rock stone . . .

Another song we used to sing was:

Ethiopian story was hidden in the dark
Nobody ever tell it to me
Ethiopian story was hidden in the dark
Ethiopian story was hidden in the dark
It's only Leonard, it's only Leonard
It's only Leonard tell it to me . . .

The girls would keep rhythm by clapping their hands, front and behind and to the side, while singing along.

Hopscotch was another crowd favorite. The girls played *Jacks*, marbles, and skipped rope, while the boys had more macho games. One popular game was *Kite Line*: you attached a razor blade to the tail of your kite, then put it up in the air and tried to cut someone else's kite. It was war—kite war! Sometimes you would make a beautiful kite and another child would cut it loose and you'd watch it drift off. The ever-present wind would blow it away and you wouldn't be able to retrieve it, so you'd have to make a new one. We were skilled, though, and could build another kite in no time. They were elaborate and colorful; we used thin bamboo sticks for the frame and paper that we got from a shop—big sheets of every color. We called it "pretty paper" even though it was used for war.

Cricket was my very favorite game. On holidays, we would get up as early as seven in the morning and spend the entire day in the sun playing cricket until dusk. I spent so much time outside that my hair turned totally red. Monty would play too, though once he started riding motorcycles—when he was quite young, even for a youth in Jamaica—he would leave for Kingston and be gone for the entire day.

In the early fifties, Baba Tewari, an acquaintance of my father, built the first movie theater in Jamaica, the Majestic, on Spanish Town Road. Some of the boys would ride their bicycles to go see a movie there. I rode with them twice when I was only nine. Starting out from Pinnacle, we'd be a big group—about twenty of us. As we rode on, we'd break up into smaller groups and I'd end up being the last one at the back. Both times I was rescued by an older youth; once it was a nice boy named Merryman, one of Brother Barrett's sons; the other time it was Bunny. For a nine-year-old child, this ride was too much. But a year later, I could ride behind Monty on his 250cc BSA motorbike; we would go to the movies in Kingston and return late at night. When I was eleven, Monty got a 650cc BSA Golden Flash, and I inherited his old 250cc BSA. We were the only kids at Pinnacle with motorbikes.

We always had pocket money. Some of us youngsters started gambling, playing *Penny Poker* and *Pit-a-Pat,* but my father had a strange habit that became an additional source of income for us. To this day, I don't know if it was an offering or superstition, but he would often throw a handful of coins out of the back window of our house. If you go up there now, I guarantee you'll find some money. We would go digging around for coins anytime we needed extra spending cash. But gambling was something Dada always warned us against, like drinking and rowdy behavior: "Don't become a gambler or a drunkard!" So all of us guys felt like fearless conspirators when we met at night in East Avenue to play *Penny Poker.* The adults turned a blind eye.

We also fought among ourselves. Two guys would slug it out, swinging at each other's mouths and noses. It was like:

"Who's king of the hill?"

"I can beat you!"

"No, you can't beat *me*!"

"Yes I can!"

I was usually the youngest boy there, and when I would win, everyone would shout, "Blade beat so-and-so, he's king of the hill!" The excitement was so electrifying that there were even twin boys named Abdulla and Zanas Sutherland who repeatedly fought each other for *King of the Hill* glory. No matter who the victor was, his name and new title would be chanted by all of us. After the fight we'd be friends again, and none of our parents would ever hear a word about it.

By age fourteen, I began making friends in Kingston and spending more time there. Some of my friends at Pinnacle must have resented it but no one ever said anything to me.

We all loved going to Kingston. Monty and I often visited Dada there, accompanied by Tatelyn and Brother Walker, one of Dada's lieutenants. To our young minds, Kingston was all excitement because there was so much to see. I remember staying at a hotel on King Street, near King George VI Memorial Park (now named National Heroes Park). You could see all kinds of flowers and neatly trimmed bushes and hedges. Large white swans and flamingos roamed among the weeping willows with branches that almost touched the ground. There were nicely dressed ladies with parasols strolling around, and sometimes a brightly uniformed military big band played in the background. To me, King George Park was the second most beautiful place on earth. The first was Hope Gardens, with its zoo that had so many incredible animals.

ENTERTAINMENT

||||||||||||||||||||||||||||||||||||||||||||||||||||||||||||||||||||||||||||||||||||

I n the early 1940s, boys would gather at night at a place we called Parade to play drums and sing. This probably continued into the early fifties. We had some very talented people, like Brother Barrett and Brother Marshall (a poet who sometimes wrote for the *Gleaner*), who made up lyrics and put them to music, or mixed them with church songs or Jamaican tunes playing on the radio at the time. Quite a lot of songs were written just for Pinnacle people, and everyone would sing them together. Some of these lyrics you can still hear today, such as, *"Leonard seeks me, Leonard finds me, he fills my heart with joy, glory alleluia, I am free!"*

In the early days, the drummers would be playing until very late, but after a while people asked them to stop earlier on weekdays because they needed to sleep. Some worked as far away as the Caymanas Estate and had to wake up at four o'clock in the morning to get there. But during holidays and festivals, everybody put up with the noise, because when those guys got on their drums, they PLAYED! I've never heard any other music like that.

On different occasions, we had parties at the big house. A lot of people would gather—we'd cook a great deal of food, play drums, dance, and make merry. One of these celebrations was Harvest, a traditional Afro-Jamaican event not exclusive to Pinnacle. These celebrations were somewhat religious but were not like regular public holidays. They were among the best experiences of my young life at Pinnacle. My favorite entertainment has always been happy gatherings of people enjoying each other's company.

Sometimes my father would give a welcoming address, other times he was away in Kingston. When he was home for a celebration, he would update everyone about the land dispute or other pressing issues, and he also gave impromptu inspirational speeches. Everyone would listen with rapt attention, but for me, because I was so young, they were just words going over my head. I was more interested in the drums, the food, and the dancing and running around with my friends.

Dada used to say, "Worship should never be joyless." When I had to leave a celebration early, I would go home and lie in my bed late at night listening to the chanting, singing, drumming, guitars, mouth organs (harmonicas), and fifes. I could listen to all of it forever. Even from my bedroom in the big house, I could hear all the sounds coming from East Avenue.

* * *

Most of the drums were made at Pinnacle. Some people brought drums with them when they moved in, but over the years these got damaged and had to be repaired or replaced. There were drum-making facilities at Pinnacle, and even someone who could build violins. There were the bass drum, the kibandu, the playing drum, the barrel, and the talking drum, which was like a kete, a repeater. We didn't have the kind you hold under your armpit; our drums were always placed on the ground and drummers would sit on them, like in Kumina. Most of the musicians came from St. Thomas, where Kumina was prevalent. Kumina is an Afro-Jamaican style of relatively recent origin. At Pinnacle, it was our main musical influence. Kingston drummers were rooted in a different African style called Burru, which had survived through slavery. We had no interaction with Count Ossie's drummers—each group tended to keep to themselves—but reggae would take inspiration from both Kumina and Burru.

Going to a Nine-Night in Pinnacle was one of the most joyous occasions I can remember. The ninth night after someone dies is a big event in Jamaica: much singing and food, playing cards, dominoes, live music—like a big party. We would stay up until dawn telling stories. A couple of times, some guys from Kingston brought their electric guitars. It was around '46 or '47, before rock and roll got started; no one there had ever seen an electric guitar before. They didn't work very well because we didn't have regular electricity up there, and batteries ran down quickly. But at first, those electric guitars really blew people's minds.

Brother Barrett was from St. Thomas and was, in my opinion, the best guitar player on earth. Even better than the ones you would hear on the radio back then. Sadly, Brother Barrett died without ever being recorded. He was so talented, and there's nothing left of his musical legacy.

MYSTIC

||||||||||||||||||||||||||||||||||||||||||||||||||||||||||||||||||||||||||||||||||||||||||

M y father was a mystic. He would meditate, read lots of books on philosophy, and he was always trying to solve problems—he was always working at *something*. He was a deep thinker, though I could not fathom many of his reflections since I was just a kid.

Dada came from a Christian background. At Pinnacle, there were Christians, Hindus, and Buddhists living in good harmony, the way it should always be. My father, like the prophet Muhammad, did not reject the Bible. As with Muslims, who believe in the Book but interpret it differently, he accepted and respected the values of Christianity.

The concept of Babylon comes from the Bible. Babylon is the source of all evil, and Zion is the *higher ground*. The British Empire was still powerful at the time, so England was considered the leader of Babylon. The colonial government and their enforcers were also Babylon, but not every individual on the outside was. The Pope was Babylon—he backed slavery and the colonization of Africa. There was still Christ, but he was used by Babylon to justify their wicked behavior, even going so far as to change his physical appearance to match their European standards of beauty. I can understand that people pray to a god that looks like them—but forcing other races to worship that same god or else suffer dire consequences is too much. I'm a firsthand seeker; I cannot believe in a god who someone else decided was a god. Dada was the one who said that Emperor Selassie was divine. Perhaps he got the idea of a Living God from the Indians—he had many Indian friends.

My father was not antagonistic to Christianity, though some Christians were very antagonistic to him, and to anything else that was not Christian. One of these people was our neighbor, Joseph Watt. Whenever he saw Monty or me, he would preach to us about God and how wrong our father was. He was one of those people who would beat you over the head with messages from the Bible. It is this oppressive side of Christianity that we rejected, not the faith itself. Piety should not be disrespectful of another person's belief. In the year 325, three centuries after Jesus died, Christianity was transformed into a political tool by Roman emperor Constantine, and it became a very powerful religion. However, it was forced on people almost like a weapon. When Christianity ruled, the world went through a dark age. Scientific knowledge was submitted to censors; anything contradicting Church teachings was suppressed. When Galileo announced that the sun doesn't revolve around the earth, as the Church claimed, he almost lost his life. Anywhere in the world you look, you can find a fanatic who believes that their way is the *only* way. My father's teaching that a Black man was God in the flesh was not something authorities were willing to accept.

Many of the things my father did seemed mysterious to people. Some of those who didn't subscribe to his views thought that he was putting a spell on people to get into their minds, or pouring some kind of drug into their drinks. Indeed, I would overhear people saying things to my father like, "You got the people to believe that a man like you is a god, you must have some extra powers." In rural St. Thomas, how could he bring hundreds of people together—not for just one night, but night after night after night? The authorities were getting jumpy: *What the hell is going on?* Dada was indeed a talented herbalist, but I believe it was primarily his personality that attracted people to him.

Reports were made to the authorities time and again accusing Dada of being an obeahman. Practicing obeah (the Jamaican brand of African magic, or sorcery, as the British would say) was a crime in Jamaica, and was severely punished by colonial laws. Throughout my entire time at Pinnacle, I heard outside people saying that my father was practicing obeah. But in *The Promised Key*, my father clearly stated his aversion to it by endorsing this quotation from the *Holy Piby*: "King Alpha says that the Balm Yard is not a hospital, neither is it an obeah shop. People who are guilty of obeah must not visit Balm Yards, nor in the assembly of Black Supremacy . . ."

Obeah is still practiced in Jamaica today. I don't think there is anything substantial to it, though I have never spent time researching or studying it. My father was of an older generation, however, and in those days, obeah was a force in Jamaican culture. I don't think Dada believed in it, but sometimes I suspected that he might have known more about it than he was willing to say.

There was a big cave in the hills that we called the Sanctuary. Early in the life of Pinnacle, Dada would go off and spend time there. I don't know what he was doing—perhaps smoking, perhaps having private time with a lady. All we knew was that sometimes he spent whole days at the Sanctuary. As far as I was concerned, he was just recharging his batteries, camping out. He had a back-to-nature spirit, something I have inherited from him, and my daughter from me.

One thing I do know: my father did not do life rituals. People in Pinnacle sometimes did such things on their own because their grandmothers were from Africa, and they wanted to keep some traditions alive from the village or region they came from. On Ethiopian holidays such as Harvest or (Ethiopian) Thanksgiving, there were sacrificial rituals and some processions too. Since there were many meat eaters at Pinnacle, they would sacrifice fowls or goats while mumbling words like, "Thank you for giving up your life so we can receive the sustenance and energy that give us the power to do Jah-Jah's work here on earth." Then they would either chop off the head or wring the neck and cook the meat for the feast.

Sacrifice was not part of my father's teachings, but there were never any big controversies over religious or spiritual practices at Pinnacle. Many people would read the Bible, the Ten Commandments, the Proverbs; some of these verses certainly have truth in them. Human values should be pretty much the same in all major religions, and this is what my father tried to instill above all else. Because of him, we knew the right way to live with one another. We had manners and respect even when none was shown to us.

Dada would always say: "Show respect to all. You cannot expect to be respected until you respect others." This was very important to him. The more respect you show other people, the more respect you can demand from them—and vice versa. "Be respectful of all, regardless of their situation in life": that was drilled into us. Disrespect was not tolerated. You had to be polite. Rastas did not use bad words—my father didn't approve of that type of language. Behave yourself, respect yourself, it all goes from there.

I would go so far as to say that Pinnacle ran on the fuel of good manners. Dada saw wisdom and a higher consciousness in Eastern philosophy, and Gandhi was one of his heroes. We sometimes need other people to help us in our search for ourselves. Dada followed that old mysticism of prefects or gurus or whatever you want to call them, and he was a strong believer in karma: what you do to others will somehow come back to you. Most Pinnacle people were of the same mentality.

Pinnacle would be a fascinating field for psychologists to study—to see how poor people can live together without problems, in peaceful coexistence with each other. There were no police or security forces, no stoplights, no punishments (except for misbehaving children). If you did something that the society thought was wrong, they would let you know with their attitudes. Through gentle behavior, people were persuaded to follow a righteous path. People wanted to fit in, that's human nature; they didn't want to appear vulgar.

In 1951, a beardman called Whoppy King, a well-known criminal, was caught and eventually hanged for murder and rape. During his very long trial, he was never mistaken for a Rasta; people only viewed him as a "beardman." My father's people did not have any physical attributes that would make them stick out in a crowd; they were hardly noticed and blended in with everyone else. The only exception was an ideology—Rasta pride! That is basically what brought Rasta teachings to Back-o-Wall and other areas of Kingston: our people were very poor, yet they were not cowed by the authorities. The thinking was, *We are a great people, and we don't bow down to Babylon.* Everyone at Pinnacle had dignity, everyone had something within him- or herself that they could share with others.

This was the "face" of Rasta in the 1950s.

HURRICANE CHARLEY

||||||||||||||||||||||||||||||||||||||||||||||||||||||||||||||||||||||||||||||||||||||||||

In January 1951, when I was nine years old, my father and his chief lieutenant at that time, Edgar Reid, were arrested in Kingston and charged with possession of ganja. Both were sentenced to a year in prison. In August, while Dada was still away, Jamaica was hit by a fierce storm, Hurricane Charley. Almost every year, Jamaica is on the natural path of various storms big and small, but Hurricane Charley was the worst. There was great destruction and many lives were lost throughout the island.

During the hurricane, I was scared out of my mind. At our house on the top of the hill, up above everything else, the storm was ferocious. Inside, you could hear the house being taken apart piece by piece. We didn't realize how lucky we were to be uninjured until the next morning when we came out and saw the level of damage. Huge trees had toppled like they were pieces of a dollhouse. Part of the roof was gone and from inside we could see straight through to the clear sky. We had been in the back of the house when the main beam fell, a twelve-by-twelve piece of wood running thirty or forty feet; when it hit the ground, it sounded like the walls had exploded. We thought the house had split in two.

But the real disaster was in East Avenue, where almost every house was destroyed. They had not been constructed to withstand violent storms. For the first time in our history, the people of Pinnacle were offered help from the outside, and we gladly accepted it. Mr. Max Henzell, father of filmmaker Perry Henzell (who years later made the movie *The Harder They Come*), was the general manager of the Caymanas sugar estate where a lot of our people worked. He demonstrated great generosity by giving our community two of the largest canvas tents I've ever seen. Those tents housed all the women and children of the compound until the men could rebuild the houses. Thankfully, despite the destruction, not one life was lost at Pinnacle.

GANJA

||||||||||||||||||||||||||||||||||||||||||||||||||||||||||||||||||||||||||||||||||||

After my father's one-year prison sentence in 1951, indictments for ganja possession and distribution became a recurring form of harassment against Rastas who used it in their meditations.

Although ganja might have been present on the island in ancient times (so much worldwide indigenous history has been erased that one can only surmise), smoking it was taught to Jamaicans by the travelers and seamen of the 1930s. The herb had been common in Harlem during the roaring twenties. Some writers, however, have linked the spread of ganja in Jamaica to an earlier set of travelers. In the nineteenth century, just after slavery, the indentured Indian people brought their religion and culture, including ganja, which they used as a sacrament in some of their rituals. St. Thomas, with its green valleys and large Indian community, became the major producer of "Kali weed" in Jamaica.

Not every Howellite smoked or planted ganja.

Some had been smoking it earlier in life, and when they moved to Pinnacle in the 1940s, they continued growing their own herb. I now know that my father smoked, but he didn't have anything to do with the ganja trade. He did not plant it, he did not sell it, and he did not command people to do it. After Hurricane Charley, the ganja planters on Pinnacle had a very good crop. The following year was even better, so they went crazy and planted a lot more.

In 1953, when large quantities were being sold, Dada might have received some gifts from the proceeds, but we never spoke about it—I was only eleven. I would watch sometimes when a truck would arrive and men would start loading bags upon bags of ganja into it. There was big business going on and Pinnacle people were becoming even more financially independent. Brother Powell, one of the people in charge of the operation, was able to buy a car. He was a very knowledgeable and sensible guy. While people in Kingston were more wrapped up in capitalist business practices—buying a product for cheap and making huge profits on its resale—Powell and his friends took good care of the cultivators who grew the plants. Powell understood that collaboration and fairness were crucial to that kind of ecosystem.

I don't know who the direct buyers were. As a child, I was not curious about things like that. I knew that some Indians were involved, including a group called Kapatula, but I didn't know anyone's names. Sometimes I wondered who ran that business, who could afford to buy sixty large crocus bags of ganja. It must have been done from very high up. Who had that kind of money?

Driving at night during that period, you would pass a police vehicle quietly parked on the side of the road, then you'd hear gossip around Pinnacle that a large sale had gone down. For some time, no one interfered with whatever business was taking place. Unfortunately, the end soon came to the short-lived ganja trade and, more importantly, life as we knew it at Pinnacle.

PART III

BABYLON SYSTEM

SHAKEDOWNS

||||||||||||||||||||||||||||||||||||||||||||||||||||||||||||||||||||||||

The police would make frequent raids or "visits" to our home in Pinnacle. I can personally remember sixteen of these.

There were two types of raids: official raids and freelance raids or shakedowns. The official raids were led by white British officers looking for "subversive activities." Every scrap of paper in the house and all our books would be confiscated. Sometimes gold cuff links, watches, and money would disappear too. During the shakedowns, however, there was no pretense of a search. Police officers would show up and say, "Oh, we just come to make sure everybody is fine. How is everything going?" And Dada would send someone over to East Avenue and one of his lieutenants would return to the house carrying an envelope with money in it. The envelope would be given to a guy everyone called "Sergeant Major," "Major," or "Sarge." This man, Sarge, was a terror, a tyrant, and a villain.

At that time in Jamaica, no Black person had ever

held a rank above sergeant, but in 1951, Jamaica promoted its first Black policeman to be a sub-inspector or assistant. Sarge would have been one of the highest-ranking Black people in the police department, where all the officers were British white men. Sarge had a lot of interaction with us over the years. He would beat up people and take away their goods. He was like a colonial master and would even assault people in the street. He was sometimes called a "flunky"—one of those Black people who supported the British and were willing to do anything to maintain the status quo: accepting the white men as their rulers. Pinnacle people despised Sarge.

I remember one day when he and several other policemen came up to the great house, and Dada sent someone over to East Avenue with a message to one of his lieutenants, Walker or Marshall, to bring the usual envelope. While we waited, some of our people came over to find out what was happening and Dada ordered a goat to be killed and cooked. The envelope arrived and was given to Sarge, then we all had a large meal: runcus soup, curry goat, and white rice. After Sarge had his fill, he went over to my father's favorite chair and sat in it.

Now, this was a very special chair. It was a rather large and expensive padded armchair that was only used by Dada—it was like his throne in the reception room. Sarge was the biggest and fattest police officer I'd ever seen, and after sitting down, he pulled out a huge cigar, lit it, and started puffing. Then he put his

feet up while pushing back on the chair . . . and *snap!*
One of the large wooden rear legs broke under his
enormous weight. Dada was mad but controlled his
emotions.

Sergeant Major's death was not mourned by many
people at Pinnacle, though it did shock the island. He
was shot by a young police officer nicknamed Bogus
Boy. Bogus Boy was probably having troubles within
the police department and went on a shooting spree,
killing several of his fellow officers, including Sarge. A
popular song came out of that incident and became a
hit on Jamaican radio:

> *They tell Bogus Boy fi go cut backra cane*
> *And that was the thing that get pon him brain,*
> *now*
> *Bend down low, for Bogus Boy a come*
> *Bend down low now, Bogus Boy a go shoot*
> *them down*
> *Bend down low, Bogus Boy a come . . .*

Although Dada did have friends in the police
force, the shooting had nothing to do with us.

Sometimes, Dada was tipped off about impending
raids and we were able to hide things. Other times,
we were taken by surprise.

The roads entering the back of Pinnacle were narrow tracks with forests on both sides; large groups
had to walk in a single file up the hill. Partway up

that hill lived a family with a clear view of the path leading up from the entrance. One night, in the dark stillness, the family heard the commotion of a large group coming up the hill and started throwing stones and shouting at the intruders. Other people in the settlement heard the family's shouts and began making noise too. Soon, everyone was screaming and throwing stones at the invaders. Those shouts, coming from all different directions of that small community within Pinnacle, confused the intruders, and they ran away. The next day in Spanish Town, people were spreading rumors that three hundred policemen had tried to assault Pinnacle from the rear and were "driven back by savages." But no shots were fired, and nobody was arrested or tried for it, though we always remained curious about who that group was.

What was that raid all about? Why did they come in from the back? Perhaps they were thieves? No, thieves would not have caused such a scandal—this raid looked like a foiled military assault.

My father told the people never to fight back, since the police were the law. What people did most of the time was sing. When the police were searching their houses, they would start in on one of those Rasta chants, hymns, or slogans, like, "*Jah Rastafari, King of Kings, Lord of Lords, Conquering Lion of the Tribe of Judah, the Light of this world and the Elect of God.*"

A lot of the songs were deep, full of good teachings, strong morals, lessons you could take power from; it was another way of praying. I recall a very old one, a sort of Rasta prayer, *"Allah, Alpha, Obanameni akoro de, yanso yanso"* . . . I never knew its origin, and I haven't heard it since I left Pinnacle. There were lots of those prayers or ritual songs—they were not sung all the time, but people knew them and would sing them when there was trouble. This would happen in the village whenever there was a raid, and the authorities would always be mystified by all those people just singing together.

THE 1954 GANJA RAID

On May 22, 1954, at four o'clock in the morning, we heard cars coming up the road, and then a heavy stampede of boots and pounding on the door. "Police!"

My father was away in Kingston at the time and Tatelyn was the only adult at home with Monty and me. At twelve and fourteen years old, we were both wearing expensive watches that our father had given us for our birthdays, so the police arrested us on "suspicion of possessing unlawful goods."

It was a very scary scene. Eight or nine Black policemen and two white British officers escorted Monty and me from our home on the hill to East Avenue, where a multitude of other people were being arrested as well. On the way, the police asked us questions and demanded that our responses be either "Yes sir" or "No sir." I complied but Monty refused to use the word "sir." His stubbornness infuriated them.

Four or five policemen rushed over and grabbed my brother. They held him by his pant waist and pushed and pulled him by his shoulders, raising their sticks as if they were about to smash in his head, shouting, "'Yes SIR'! Mi sey, sey it!"

I kept begging Monty to give in, but he steadfastly refused. I thought we were going to get beaten or killed. I'd never been so terrified in my life. Eventually, one of the white officers told the Black policemen to stop. They never did get that "sir" out of Monty's mouth. Was it bravery or foolhardy stubbornness? I still cannot decide.

When we got to East Avenue, we saw hundreds of our people—men, women, and even some children—helplessly standing in queues waiting to be booked. A lot of ganja had been found on the property and in some people's homes, but not everyone arrested had taken part in the planting, growing, selling, or even the smoking of it. One by one, each person had to walk up to a table where another policeman was sitting and give their name. The police were not interested in knowing whether people were involved with ganja or not, they simply told them that they were under arrest for possession of a pound or two. I remember a sixteen-year-old girl, Christine, who was very frightened. She didn't have anything to do with ganja—she didn't even smoke cigarettes—but she was arrested all the same.

Monty and I were taken in a "Black Mariah" police van to the Spanish Town police station on Young Street. A message was sent to my father through a Thompson Pen grocery store owner: if he did not pay

£500 sterling, Monty and I would be charged with having a pound of ganja in our possession. They were extorting my father, and he couldn't do anything about it.

Over four hundred people were arrested during the raid. At the trial, the judge didn't listen to the "not guilty" pleas and sentenced more than three hundred Pinnacle people to prison for one year, even Christine. Some received hard labor.

Dada paid the extortion money and the ganja charges never materialized for Monty and me. The unlawful possession charges were still pending, but my father obtained copies of the original receipts from Wright's Jewelry Store on King Street where he had bought the watches. Those receipts were presented to the court and the unlawful possession charges were finally dropped, as reported in the *Gleaner* on June 12, 1954: "No Case Against Howell's Sons." Our names were spelled incorrectly.

To this day, I still don't know who the mastermind was behind that raid. It could have simply been a rival group of planters. All kinds of people were planting herbs; we were not the only ones. But that wasn't the point. A message had gone out that the only thing we were doing up at Pinnacle was planting ganja—and that was all it took. It was the biggest ganja raid in Jamaican history up to that point and the government used it as an excuse to cripple an entire community. The authorities had what they wanted: an opportunity to get rid of the Rastas.

* * *

Although we went on living there, Pinnacle never fully recovered from that raid. A lot of key people had been arrested and put in prison, and there was still so much work left to do. In 1955, my father declared bankruptcy and all our vehicles and machinery were seized. Then, a year later, the authorities finally found a way to permanently remove my family from Pinnacle.

Since Pinnacle's inception, my father had always wanted the land to be registered in the name of the Ethiopian Salvation Society. I have governmental letters that reveal the debate over the legitimacy of the organization, as well as the attorney general's statement in 1944 to the honorable colonial secretary that Pinnacle belonged to my father. However, with Albert Chang's death in 1946, *proving* ownership became a bigger problem.

No one ever knew what happened to the original agreement Chang made with my father. If there were any receipts for the transactions between Dada and Chang, they were most likely confiscated, stolen, or destroyed in one of the raids or shakedowns, along with most of Dada's writings and possessions. There were also suspicious fires at the Spanish Town courthouse and the Island Records Office in Spanish Town that would have housed any documentation of Pinnacle's ownership. Unbeknownst to any of us at the time, and despite my father paying taxes on the land, the title of the land was being manipulated by several outside people and entities.

Rumors would later spread that after Chang's death, Pinnacle was bestowed to the Boy Scouts Association, then to Edward Rasheed Hanna, and then finally to Joseph Linton Watt. There were probably more people involved than we will ever know. But neither the Boy Scouts nor Hanna ever contacted us or made any visible move against the settlement while they were the "registered owners."

Dada had been spending a lot of time in Kingston trying to straighten out the ownership problem when we lost everything. Monty was running an errand, so I was alone in the house with just a helper on that fateful day in 1956. About a dozen policemen and an equal number of civilians drove up to our place. The intruders read what they alleged to be an eviction order signed by Joseph Watt, my father's archenemy. He claimed to have bought the Pinnacle property from Edward Hanna and stated that "Howell and his two sons are to vacate the premises at once." Decades later, Joseph Watt's son, Joe Samuel, would say in a 1998 interview with French journalist Hélène Lee that his father told him he had bought the land from Dada.

The police and their helpers proceeded to load our furniture, clothing, and all our earthly possessions onto a trailer, and a tractor pulled it down to the main gate and dumped it onto the road. They had to make several trips. Everything was left in front of the main gate, so that anyone could come and take whatever they wanted.

Nothing had ever worried me at Pinnacle. You could run in any direction, there was space to jump and scream and shout . . . but now the authorities were telling me that I had to go. The day I left in 1956, I felt as if my life was over. I was fourteen years old and the paradise that was my birthplace and home had been stolen right from under me.

DARK YEARS

‖‖

When my father lost Pinnacle, he lost his foundation. We were back in the outside world and homeless. In the space of three years, my brother and I moved five times.

That first day, I went to Kingston and stayed with Pearl Staniger, the mother of four of my siblings. After a few days, I was reunited with Monty and he took me to Thompson Pen, where he had rented a room from Mrs. Isaacs, the mother of a friend; we stayed with her for about nine months. When we left, we rented a proper house in Kingston at 10 Arlington Avenue in Vineyard Town. Then Monty and I moved to Tatley Avenue, off Maxfield Avenue in Kingston, and after that to Port Antonio.

While we were still shuffling around, looking for permanent lodging and mourning our lost paradise, Pinnacle tried to go on surviving, even without Dada. There were still anywhere from eight hundred to a thousand people living in East Avenue alone. But from 1957–58, the villages and even the cottage I was born and raised in were set on fire and burned to the ground by the order of Joseph Watt. In that same 1998 interview mentioned earlier, Joe Samuel corroborated this fact. Of course, we did not know for sure at the time that it was him, but we had our suspicions. Our friends Abdulla and Zanas Sutherland had been working on Watt's property and claimed to have witnessed Prime Minister Bustamante visiting him on several occasions.

There was no mention in any newspapers of the fire, the total and complete destruction of a community, or the overnight displacement of four thousand poor people. Considering how much press Dada and the Rastas had received over the years, it was shocking that there was no media coverage of these devastating events. No sympathy was sought, and no empathy was given. The media silence could have only come from the top down. Authorities no longer wanted Rastas to receive any attention, especially since their leader had already been removed from his land. In subsequent years, there have been no lectures discussing reparations for those who were forced to flee from the fire based on one man's greed. And even now, as I write this, few people still living on the property know the real story of how Pinnacle was stolen from my father and his followers, and how there have been efforts to erase an entire movement from Jamaican history.

The displacement, however, backfired on the authorities in an unforeseeable way. Instead of being self-contained and isolated to one location, Pinnacle people were now dispersed all over the island. Mainstream society had no choice now but to engage with the Rastas who the media had portrayed as hooligans and ruffians. The new communities were not always welcoming, and without a centralized leader, many of Dada's followers became bitter and angry, and the image and culture of Rasta began to radically change. Many new groups emerged, claiming they were Rastas, and in Kingston an entirely new Rasta generation was brewing. I did not pay attention to the different sects, though. Life after Pinnacle was so devastating that my own daily survival was my primary concern.

A large portion of Pinnacle people settled in nearby Tredegar Park, a suburb of Spanish Town, under the leadership of Sister Gertrude Campbell, my father's last lieutenant, and many still live there today. Others, including Dada, settled in the foothills of Pinnacle. He built a small house in the wilderness and eventually opened another bakery to feed the surrounding community.

In 1959, Monty and I moved back to Kingston, and Belmont Road became Monty's last address in Jamaica before he moved to England to escape the constant harassment we were all enduring.

One afternoon, Monty was riding his motorcycle back from the foothills of Pinnacle where he had been visiting our father. Approaching the Ferry police station, halfway to Kingston, someone signaled him to stop. His Norton 1,000cc Black Shadow was the fastest vehicle in Jamaica at the time, so at first he ignored the signal and kept on going, but then he decided to turn around. A plainclothes policeman approached and ordered him to the nearby guard room to be searched: he was suspected of carrying ganja. Certain that once he was inside the station, the police would claim that they found something on him, Monty said, "No, search me right here!" The policeman immediately switched the motorcycle off and put the key in his pocket, while a small group of onlookers gathered around. For Monty, this was an extremely dangerous situation and he had to think fast. He suddenly ripped open his shirt, turned out his pockets, and dropped his pants right there, declaring in a loud voice, "As all can see, I have nothing on my person." The police had no choice but to let him go.

With the constant threats Monty was receiving from the police, he knew that sooner or later something was going to happen to him, and he decided to relocate to England. At this time, public opinion was really starting to turn against us. It was truly the worst time of my life.

In 1960, a man named Claudius Henry, who claimed to be a Rasta, attempted an armed rebellion against the authorities. He was not from our movement, and I personally heard him on several occasions cursing my father on the radio, accusing him of making false prophecies and issuing other ridiculous statements. I wish I could find a recording of these programs to show just how misguided this man was. But his lambasting did not last long. Soon, he was in serious trouble. The police put an informer in Henry's midst, a guy called "Thunder." Henry's people found out and killed the man. (It was a popular joke that when someone would ask, "Where is Thunder?" they would be told: "We don't know, but Thunder don't roll no more!") After Henry's people murdered two British soldiers, the government launched a huge manhunt to catch them. Four were hanged, including Henry's son.

I never met anyone from Claudius Henry's movement—we had no interaction—but since he claimed to be a Rasta, we were being judged in the same light. Yet Rastas were not killers! There might have been cases of beardmen killing people, but not Rastas. A Rasta would use persuasion, ideas, philosophy—anything but violence.

Being born and raised in Pinnacle gave me unparalleled insight into the true paradise that Rastas sought. So when I saw the violence that was taking place in Kingston, I knew these men were not Rastas. They were hooligans! Every human being should know who he or she is, and Henry thought he was a Rasta, but he was totally alien to our group and to my father's teachings. The movement Henry started supported military tactics and attacked the government with guns. My father did not believe in using guns against other humans. He wanted to change things through intellectual persuasion, so that people could decide for themselves: *This course is right, this is what I am going to do.* Rasta is supposed to be a mind-expanding perspective, not just some idea of "God." You're a special entity in the universe, with a solid set of values: get up, be independent, don't believe that someone else is going to do anything for you—do it for yourself.

But my father no longer had a way to make his voice heard. After Pinnacle was taken from him, he shunned publicity and never gave interviews. People were telling lies about him every day and he would not refute them. I'm ashamed to admit this, but it was embarrassing to watch his fall from grace. Newspapers could write whatever they wanted and he would not come out and defend himself. He was, however, very upset by the turn of events. He looked at the Henry foolishness and the killings with disdain. It hurt his sense of humanity since he was always consciously fighting for the little man. That's how he saw his role in life. He was not thinking of Rasta as his own local thing, he was thinking globally, he wanted to expand his vision to the world. He told me on several occasions to change the name of our organization from the Ethiopian Salvation Society to the Ethiopian *Worldwide* Salvation Society. He was adamant about it with Monty and me: "This is *your* thing now!" My father always expected Monty to be his primary heir, but my brother soon left for England and would be gone for a decade. So now my father bestowed me with the charge. But at that time, there was so much uncertainty in my life that I was simply trying to survive.

In Kingston, I did not know anyone from Pinnacle except for my other siblings and their respective mothers, Pearl, Ivy, and Olive Malavre. But I eventually met and grew close to people from my mother's side of the family, including Aunt B. Lynch and my Uncle Ned Bent and his family.

I made many good new friends, and I felt safe with them, but Pinnacle and Kingston were two very different worlds. I never discussed Pinnacle with people outside of Pinnacle; I never told people who I was—though some of them knew. I heard whispering in the street: "A Gong son dat!" "A Gong son, you know!" It was so unnerving. In certain circles, Dada was still regarded as a monster who disemboweled his wife, as well as a drug dealer, a lunatic, a tyrant posing as God. No voice rose to defend his cause. Even with girlfriends, I would not openly reveal who I was. I remember dating one young woman until her father found out who my father was and forbade her from seeing me. I eventually applied to and enrolled in the Jamaica School of Art and Crafts in 1959, where I studied painting and sculpture before finally settling on commercial art, which became my profession.

No longer having a large following, my father now lived humbly. When he visited Kingston, he would stay with me or on South Camp Road, where he had a room at a friend's boardinghouse. It was a big structure, two or three stories tall; from its flat roof, you could look down into Sabina Park, one of cricket's most famous grounds, where world records were made and broken.

In 1962, Jamaica achieved independence from England, and Alexander Bustamante became prime minister. He lost no time in taking his revenge on Rastafari, "the most dangerous thing in this country." The Coral Gardens incident in 1963 provided him with the opportunity to come down hard on Rastas.

The story I heard was that someone named Beardman Gardener from Montego Bay had an altercation with the police and was shot and left for dead. But after heavy surgery and a long stay in the hospital, he survived. When he came out, suffering and diminished, he decided to retaliate. Along with a few accomplices, he attacked several civilians and police, killing at least two people, and burned down a gas station. He was eventually caught in a police ambush and shot to death.

Bustamante ordered mass arrests. The police had carte blanche to strike out at Rastas, and persecuted any man with long hair or a beard. Many dreadlocked Rastas were rounded up, taken to jail, and beaten, and their hair was cut; I think some died in custody. The Claudius Henry and Coral Gardens episodes did not affect the people from Pinnacle because most did not have dreadlocks and were largely inconspicuous among the general population, but several Rastas whose appearance stood out lost their lives.

* * *

One of the most important and celebrated events in Rasta and Jamaican history took place in 1966, with the visit of His Imperial Majesty Emperor Haile Selassie I of Ethiopia.

Unfortunately, we, the Howells, were never told about the visit, and were not invited to participate in any of the surrounding events. We heard about it on the radio and in the newspapers. We sent a delegation to the government to find out how we could play a role in the celebrations, but we were told that we could only have spectators' accommodations, and that we couldn't actually participate in any of the events. We sent a busload of people to Norman Manley Airport to try to welcome the emperor, but we could not get anywhere near him.

The government had officially shut Dada out.

In my final year at the Jamaica School of Art and Crafts, I interned at Lonsdale Hands, the biggest advertising agency in the country, located on Duke Street in Kingston. It was a British firm that occupied three floors of the Bernard Stanley Building, the first high-rise in Kingston. After my internship, I was asked to stay on as a full-time employee.

In 1969, I had an opportunity to move to New York City, where I accepted a job as an artist at the Jack Meyer Labeling Corporation Packaging System. I returned to Jamaica in 1970 to pick up my longtime girlfriend, Curlyn Adams, and we lived together until we got married in 1975. We settled down in the US, and for years I didn't want to look back on my life in Jamaica—remembering was too painful.

We now have two children, Steven and Ingrid, and two grandchildren, Destiny and Lion. I went back briefly to Jamaica in 1981 to settle some affairs following my father's death, but didn't return again for another twenty-eight years.

NOT AN ORDINARY
KIND OF MAN

||||||||||||||||||||||||||||||||||||||||||||||||||||||||||||||||||||||||||||||||||||||||||||

For many years, I brushed aside all memories of Pinnacle and my father. Monty and I refused all requests for interviews—we stopped trying to explain long ago. As teenagers, we learned that it was futile at best, and dangerous at worst. It took millions of reggae records to carry my father's message across the world, but it also took me decades to come to terms with the embarrassment and the bitterness, and to realize what an extraordinary person our father had been.

Dada usually wore a three-piece suit with a vest. Whenever he had a suit made, he always ordered a jacket, a vest, and two pairs of pants. Off-the-rack suits were rarely sold in Jamaican shops, everyone had them tailored—and our tailors at Pinnacle could make you a suit in no time. I remember Dada wearing an African robe a couple of times, but I don't think that was for the public. To move in certain circles, you had to fit in. Regardless, he had a very strong personality. He could argue about anything, and people would marvel at how learned he was, although he was self-educated. He could not be bullied or pushed around. He would stand his ground intellectually and was capable of changing minds. If someone did something wrong, he would not hesitate to tell them. Everyone could feel his strength. When angry, he could terrorize people in the most surprising of ways.

I remember one day in the late 1940s when we were returning to Pinnacle from Kingston and we stopped at a shop on Thomson Pen Road. When Brother Jackson went inside to buy some O-So Grape soda for Monty and me, a small crowd gathered around the car where Dada, Monty, Sister Pearl, and I sat waiting. A man holding a cane bill (a tool used to cut sugarcane) started being disrespectful to my father and insulting Rastas. Dada jumped out of the car and walked straight up to the offender—he just looked him in the eye, and the man fainted! I don't know what the hell my father did, but suddenly the man was on the ground. Dada didn't say anything afterward and we did not ask, but I am still baffled and bewildered. He was a fearless man—he'd stand up to anything.

Another time, after the big raid in 1954, I had gone to Denham Town in Kingston to visit Pearl and her children. I was playing with a bunch of kids from the neighborhood when a policeman came around the corner. All the other kids ran away, but I did not—I had no reason to. The officer grabbed me and slapped the back of my neck two or three times, then took me to the Denham Town police station.

"Book this little boy down now," the policeman said. "I come in the street, and he did not run!"

"I'm being arrested for *not* running!?" I replied. Then something strange happened when I said that I was Leonard Howell's son.

The sergeant jumped from behind his desk, almost apologizing for the officer who'd brought me in. "Oh, it's all right now, we're protecting you," he said, and then turned to the others. "This is Howell's son."

I don't know if he was sympathetic to our cause or just being a decent human. By then, a delegation of our people had arrived, and the officers let me leave with them. When I later told my father what had happened, he was mad and said he was going to hire a lawyer. But by that time, we were so broke that we couldn't afford to do that.

After losing Pinnacle, my father became a different man. The younger Dada had been a lion. He would not back down, he would not retreat. When he saw the police do something he did not approve of, he would talk to them—and they usually respected him too. But now that he had lost his land, power, and influence, there was little he could do anymore. He was still passionate and adamant about uplifting the downtrodden, yet he stopped giving public speeches. He scoured newspapers and wrote letters about justice, peace, and dignity to anyone who would read them. He challenged the papers to print the truth and not be influenced by political propaganda and bribes. Some scholars have surmised that Dada retreated into hiding, though that is not entirely true. He was still around, still advocating, still feeding the hungry and healing the sick. And he was still being harassed and silenced by the authorities. No one had ever tried to hit my father or use brute force against him when Pinnacle was in its glory days and he had thousands of followers. But when he lost everything, he was viciously attacked in his little house in the wilderness. Plots were later uncovered to disenfranchise my father from what he had created.

On January 7, 1990, journalist Richard Heller published an article with the headline "British Plotted Against Rasta" in the *Mail on Sunday*, a British newspaper. The article outlined a plot hatched in 1959 by the British and Jamaican governments to stop the growth of the Rastafarian movement in Jamaica while simultaneously negotiating with the Ethiopian government, calling for Emperor Selassie to renounce Rasta and make a public statement to the world that he was not a god.

The plan faltered for Sir Hugh Foot, the outgoing governor of Jamaica, so it was left to his successor, Sir Kenneth Blackburn, to prod the British Foreign Office into action. On June 10, 1959, Blackburn wrote to Colonial Secretary Alan Lennox-Boyd about his optimism for the Moral Rearmament Movement—the wording they used for the mission to convert the

Rastas. Their plan failed, and although Haile Selassie declared himself a Christian, he stayed silent on the question of his own divinity.

In 1980, a gang of thugs attacked my father and tried to cut out his tongue. But even then, at eighty-two years old, Dada stood his ground and came out wounded but alive. The attackers were dressed in dirty clothes and gave the appearance of being poor people. However, witnesses said that there were two articles of clothing the attackers all wore that contradicted their outward appearance: clean white undershirts and good shoes. Sister Campbell stayed by Dada's side for the next few months, and she was there with him when he died in 1981—less than a year after the attack.

I flew back to Kingston to bury my father, then cut my ties with the island that had taken so much from me.

I ended my self-imposed exile in 2009 when French writer/biographer Hélène Lee, who had published a book about my father called *The First Rasta*, invited me and Curlyn to travel to Jamaica for the making of a documentary about him.

The time had come to face my heritage.

PART IV
HIGHER GROUND

I visited Pinnacle in 2009 after many years away.

FOOD FOR THOUGHT

||||||||||||||||||||||||||||||||||||||||||||||||||||||||||||||||||||||||||||||||||||||

W hen young people question me about my father's message, I realize that although they may glorify his name, they usually have no idea what he actually stood for. The Internet does not help either: what you find there concerning Leonard Howell is wild fantasy. One example is a website that lists what they claim were my father's "six principles":

1. Hatred for the white race
2. The complete superiority of the Black race
3. Revenge on whites for their wickedness
4. The negation, persecution, and humiliation of the government and legal bodies of Jamaica
5. Preparation to go back to Africa
6. Acknowledging Emperor Haile Selassie as the Supreme Being and only ruler of Black people

My father hated no race (he has children and

grandchildren of all colors and hues), was not preparing to go back to Africa (he wanted to build a new society inside Jamaica), and when it comes to "negation, persecution, and humiliation," *we* were the ones who were persecuted and negated, not "the legal bodies of Jamaica."

From the very beginning, false information was deliberately spread by my father's enemies to sustain the idea that he was fighting for foolish, dangerous goals and that he was disrupting the peace. He was never given a chance to express his vision at the University of West Indies (UWI). In their 1960 "Report on the Rastafari Movement in Kingston," the UWI professors neglected to do proper research on Pinnacle or even interview Dada (this was many years before his death, and he lived right there in Kingston), instead relying on negative hearsay. The report gave credence to blatant falsehoods, such as: my father was a soldier in the Ashanti war; he sold the emperor's photograph as a passport to Ethiopia; at Pinnacle he had "savage dogs" and guardsmen who grew dreadlocks; he promoted repatriation to Africa; he had thirteen wives; he raided his neighbors and beat them; he declared himself a god; he was locked up again as a lunatic in 1960, etc., etc. To this day, the same untruths are reproduced from one "academic" text to the next. No one ever seems to bother checking facts with anybody who lived at Pinnacle.

Pinnacle was the embodiment of my father's philosophy and the blueprint for a Rasta society and way of life. It was my father's personality, his aura, his knowledge, and his dedication to the uplifting of the small man and woman that gave rise to a global movement. The Pinnacle experience could be a model for many tiny communities around the world trying to survive within a hostile system.

Yet none of the books I read prior to 2000 that touched upon Pinnacle gave any insight into this unique phenomenon, apart from a remarkable article by Professor Robert Hill of UCLA, "Dread History: Leonard P. Howell and Millenarian Visions in the Early Rastafarian Religion in Jamaica," published first in 1981 and then in 1983 in the *Jamaica Journal*. To my knowledge, this was the first published writing to place my father as the central figure in the story of Rasta, though it did not say much about Pinnacle. In the 1990s, there were several contributions by knowledgeable historians: Jamaican writer and scholar Louis E.A. Moyston, Kingston lawyer and publisher Ras Miguel Lorne, and professors Barry Chevannes (UWI), Horace Campbell (Syracuse University), and Jake Homiak (Smithsonian Institution), to name a few. But it was not until my coauthor Hélène Lee's highly researched book *The First Rasta: Leonard Howell and the Rise of Rastafarianism*, published in 2000, that the world could finally learn the truth of the founding of the Rasta movement.

Suddenly, the Internet had tens of thousands of entries with my father's name. Over the next few years, the University of the West Indies at Mona organized conferences, and symposiums were held in Africa, England, and other parts of the world. In my opinion, D.A. Dunkley, of UWI's Department of History and Archaeology, wrote the most historically accurate account of events surrounding Dada and Pinnacle in his 2013 article entitled "The Suppression of Leonard Howell in Late Colonial Jamaica, 1932–1954." With all this newfound attention to facts, the true value of Leonard Howell's role in the Rasta movement finally began to emerge. The light was finally beginning to shine on Dada's mission.

Rasta is still being defined—this is what I believe. When people ask me about it, all I can do is share my experience, tell Rasta as I see it. Here are some questions I am frequently asked, along with my responses:

Is Rasta for Black people only?
The poor people who built Pinnacle with my father were mostly Black, and they had to overcome hundreds of years of racial victimization. They had to be empowered, given back their pride in who they were. The international audience came to understand this, and very few people felt rebuffed by the "Black" side of the message. I was told that even Bob Dylan and John Lennon visited Pinnacle when they came to Jamaica, and today you can find Rastas among almost all the tribes on earth. Changing the name of his organization to the Ethiopian *Worldwide* Salvation Society demonstrated the inclusivity of my father's ideas and philosophy to a global audience, not just one race.

Perhaps it was the Nyabinghi who emphasized the "Black" aspect of Rasta. There are all kinds of people among the Nyabinghi group, and many of them were my friends. In fact, it was my father who first mentioned the existence of this mysterious African army allegedly raised by Emperor Selassie against white oppressors—Dada used to say that his followers were the "Nyabinghi army." Then other people took the name and began calling themselves Nyabinghis: "We are the Nyaman!" The "Nyabinghi army" was in fact a myth invented by Benito Mussolini's Italian propagandists to justify the use of mustard gas against Ethiopian civilians. Yet the idea of a secret Black army led by the emperor appealed to us. It was like an army of Black angels hovering over us, protecting us beneath their dark wings.

But we never advocated violence against any individual, creed, or nation. Although Dada was a Christian by birth and an Ethiopian Orthodox when he died, the Rasta organization he was closest to was the Twelve Tribes of Israel, which might be the most open-minded of the Rasta denominations. I do not know much about their genesis or their philosophy—that developed long after our departure from Pinnacle.

Another thing that bothers me is that some self-appointed "Rasta leaders" are mistreating foreign visitors at Pinnacle; for example, they have ostracized white women and pestered them with demands of "ritual observance." We never had any rule that women were required to wear scarves! That simply did not exist at Pinnacle. But some foreign visitors who have come from places as far away as Japan, Australia, the United States, and other parts of the world have gotten frightened and have left without seeing the land; they've been subjected to sexism and racism. Are not Africans supposed to be among the world's most hospitable people? Where are the manners and respect?

Is Rasta a religion?

There is a religious side to Rasta, but it comes mostly from the very religious mentality of Jamaica. Some people cannot relate to anything unless it has religious elements. That is in part how my father came to the understanding that the emperor was divine. People needed to relate to a Black god, not the god(s) of the white oppressors. This was part of the self-esteem reconstruction process. But not all Pinnacle people were religious. Some practiced traditional African rituals, while others came from Christian or Hindu backgrounds. My father did not disdain any religious faith. He had a lofty vision of "divinity" in which every human being should be aware that there is a higher power within themself, and it is up to the individual to find and develop it. Rasta is the better part of any human, the best part in you!

Should Black people go "back" to Africa?

The Back to Africa movement has been around for centuries. Was it not natural for enslaved people, violently removed from Africa, to want to return to their homeland? But my father had traveled and observed that the system of oppression—Babylon—was world-wide. So his priority was to secure a place within Jamaica where people could rebuild themselves. Claudius Henry, for one, was preaching a return to Africa, but my father knew that the Jamaican authorities would never let their cheap source of labor slip from their grip. And which African country—overcrowded, plagued by foreign exploitation, corruption, and religious wars—would or could admit tens of thousands of Jamaican migrants without collapsing? My father wanted to go back to Africa bearing gifts for the Africans, not to become a burden to impoverished states.

Did Leonard Howell claim to be God?
My father never even *hinted* that he was God. He thought of himself as a teacher, a counselor, and a prophet—he had a message for the world. Yet people idolized him to the point that they closely associated *him* with Emperor Selassie. Once, when I was a child, another youngster told me that my father was God; I said he was not, and the boy fell to the ground laughing: "Blade doesn't know that his father is God!"

Lowie, a Pinnacle elder, recently told me that he had many pictures of Dada. I was so excited, but what he came up with were photographs of the emperor that my father had distributed. Lowie was sad to see me disappointed: "See him there, this is him, Prince Regent!" And I realized that for Lowie, my father *was* the emperor.

I am always embarrassed when confronted with that kind of worship. Although my father's followers did not bend their knees or kiss his feet when he approached, they would nod and take off their hats. They had a profound love and respect for this man who had changed their lives. Like Jesus, he had gone through terrible tribulations to give them a place to live, grow, and strive. Even today, when you meet the old ones at Tredegar Park, you can still feel this love.

After the death of Haile Selassie in 1975, I thought some people would stop worshipping the emperor. But while gods and prophets die, their followers continue to believe. Buddha, Muhammad, and my father all departed from this world leaving a lasting legacy—as did Jesus Christ, although there is no scientific proof that he actually existed (but that is a whole other story . . .).

Did women have the same rights as men?
At Pinnacle, there was no gender discrimination, no separation between men and women. As I have said, women were not expected to wear scarves or dress in any particular way. In fact, women were the foundation of Pinnacle. In the first years, they were the majority among the Rastas. I will not dwell again on the important role played by my mother, Tenneth Bent-Howell; there were many other strong women there as well. Single women had a hard time raising their kids on the outside; at Pinnacle, at least, they did

The Bobo singers, with their striking headdresses and burning lyrics, brought some notoriety to the Bobo Ashanti community in the 1990s, but their leader, Prince Emmanuel, had a long history of tribulations dating back to the 1950s. Some people claim that he spent time at Pinnacle, but this is not true. I never met him or even heard of him there. He could have been at a remote location in Pinnacle, but I am sure he never visited East Avenue, and I don't think he had any contact with my father. Prince Emmanuel's community may have been *inspired* by Pinnacle, but his organization had nothing to do with ours. His organization was obsessively religious, had a strict set of rules, and women were segregated. They were among the "Rasta" groups that became prominent after my father's influence declined. Saddest of all, many so-called "Rasta leaders" nowadays are either uninformed or totally unaware of the history of Pinnacle and how the way of life they decree was started there.

What is the connection between Bob Marley and Rasta?
Many musicians are enlightened people, and they have a wonderful platform to promote their vision. I knew Bob Marley when I was living at Tatley Avenue in Kingston. At parties, we would dance to the music of Prince Buster, Derrick Morgan, and Bob Marley before they became world-famous. Back then, the most popular musical genre was ska, and the dancing rhythm was probably more important than the

message in the music itself. In the 1960s, ska evolved into reggae music, and the lyrics began to mimic the chants and hymns of Rastas. Bob was inspired by Rasta teachings and, like my father, tried to unite people, but through a different medium: music. His lyrics would go on to make Rasta philosophy and culture accessible to the world, which I thought fell right in line with the movement's inclusivity.

I have seen a lot of Bob's interviews, and I liked his calm, nonviolent, easygoing mind. That is the overall message: We are not here to threaten people, to convert them, or to beat them over the head so that they bow to our god. We tell them what we think is right and they—at least most—know what to do if they pay attention to their own conscience.

Bob was a brilliant poet. He didn't have a university education, but he came up with some very unique words and powerful insights. He was one of the greatest Rasta prophets ever; he really spread the word!

THE SEARCH FOR GOD

||||||||||||||||||||||||||||||||||||||||||||||||||||||||||||||||||||||||||||||||||||||||||

When I was about twelve years old, I started to seriously question all forms of religion. The concept of a single god, the basis of most modern creeds, was not working for me. One day I went to a Catholic church with some friends. At that time, Catholic mass was spoken in Latin. The priest had a golden rod in one hand and a golden chain and scepter in the other; he was burning frankincense and myrrh and saying these strange Latin words, and I was wondering, *What does all this Latin have to do with serving God? I am certain that no one in this church understands a word of what this man is saying! Why listen to words that we cannot understand?*

I was thinking a lot about God in those days. Did He, She, or It really exist? If so, He could do ANY and EVERYTHING, so I asked myself: *Could God create a stone heavier than He could lift? If so, isn't that a logical inconsistency?* And right then and there, I came to the realization that God did not create humans in His likeness: humans create gods in *their own* likeness. So very early in life I became an atheist, and I soon converted my brother. We got a book called *The Bible Unmasked* by Joseph Lewis, which was published in 1926 and revealed inconsistencies in the Bible, even taking offense at some of the stories that verged on pornography. In Genesis, God tells one man to sleep with his brother's wife, but the brother spills his semen on the ground and that displeases God, so He slays him! *What are you saying to me? Someone had a child and God made the child wicked, and because he was wicked, God slew him?* Read the Old Testament—there are some weird things in there. This god exhibits wicked behavior: when He doesn't like someone, He kills them.

Some groups now claim Rasta for themselves: "We are Jah Nation!" But I think that is wrong. No one can tell you who you are, or what to think. Rasta is not something you study or are appointed to—if you feel in your heart that you are a Rasta, then you ARE a Rasta. It is supposed to enlighten you, to make you more aware of life and of your place in it, and once you get this spark, it will guide you, make you feel the power within yourself. You can do great things if you know how to harness this power.

Rasta is enlightenment, but enlightenment does not have to be *one* thing. Some Rastas just sit and pray to the emperor, but there are ways to enlighten people without a supreme being. Personally, I do not believe there is one entity that is supreme. If there is a god, He, She, or It probably doesn't like human beings—we are the most destructive of all creatures on earth. Yet some people have ways of explaining things that *empower* you, and my father was that type of person.

I once took a course in the US called EST (Erhard Seminars Training). It was all about self-enlightenment, empowering yourself, and taking responsibility for your life. It was a big thing in New York back in the seventies and eighties. We all sat in front of the speakers for hours, doing some mind-bending/battling exercises. EST was making a fortune. The weekend seminar cost $350, a lot of money at that time. Many of the participants were young professionals working in Manhattan—lawyers, doctors, engineers, people in the advertising industry, etc. Psychologists and psychoanalysts made up the largest group. A lot of rich and famous people were in attendance. I met Christina Onassis, daughter of Aristotle Onassis, and she turned out to be a nice and funny person. We sat there listening to this philosopher Werner Erhard speaking, and suddenly it hit me: those were my father's teachings!

In the end, EST did indeed help me. For thirty-five years I worked as a commercial artist in New York City, rising from paste-up artist to art director. When I enrolled in EST, I was employed by Norman, Craig & Kummel, a large advertising agency in Midtown Manhattan. I was one of the very few Black art directors in the early 1970s. I had asked for a well-deserved raise, but my immediate bosses had turned my request down, offering a title promotion instead but no extra pay. My only recourse was to speak directly to the chief executive officer and owner of the company, Mr. Norman B. Norman—but prior to EST, I didn't have the nerve.

Among the different processes we went through at that EST Seminar, there was one designed to help rid ourselves of fears. At some point, I started laughing out loud, almost uncontrollably. My father had told me the same thing years earlier: "This is just another man like yourself, he puts his pants on one foot at a time, just like you. Why should you be afraid to go and talk to him? JUST GO DO IT!" My big problem was solved! I could not wait for Monday morning to rush into my boss's office and ask for my raise. And, sure as hell, I got a big one!

Every individual, of every creed or nation, has great powers within him- or herself, if only they know how to tap into them. Werner Erhard was heavily influenced by Hindu philosophy, but the idea was basically the same: The power is there inside of you, so you must find a way of tapping into that inner resource, that spiritual self or whatever you want to call it. The more you develop your intellect, the more society will benefit from it. The priority for my father was to give people something to eat and combat the prevailing low self-esteem and destitution. Therefore, he decided to provide land for people on which they could live and be free, so that they could become whatever they wanted to be. Pinnacle was a place where you built yourself and your society at the same time.

HIGHLIGHT OF MY LIFE

I n 2016, my wife Curlyn and I were invited by Professor Azoumana Ouattara, a dean at the Université Alassane Ouattara in the Ivory Coast, Africa, to attend an international music festival and symposium held at the Palais de la Culture in Abidjan called "ABI Reggae." It was the brainchild of Minister of State Moussa Dosso and a team of friends, all fans of Bob Marley from their student days.

Four nights of reggae concerts were staged on a large lawn on the edge of Laguna Bay, with the sea breeze blowing gently and the city lights of modern Abidjan reflecting off the calm water. It was one of the most beautiful visions one could ever imagine. Dignitaries and guests from all over the world were entertained by some of the most famous international reggae artists. The magic of the music was amplified by a state-of-the-art audio and visual system that enhanced the enchantment of the scenery at night.

During the day, panel discussions were held throughout the compound, aimed at taking a critical look at the role of reggae music, and the role that Rasta philosophy can play, in bridging the gaps between tribes. Was it possible for reggae and Rasta to push society beyond tribal disputes and ward off the menace of war? One African delegate even said to me, "Reggae heals wounds in Africa."

The festival's keynote speech focused on enslavement and restitution, and there was a panel that explored contemporary Pan-Africanism. I was invited to talk about my father's work and legacy in a panel titled, "Rastafari: A New Religion or a Way of Life?"

During the panel, Professor Ouattara and I discussed reparations and repatriation. I told him that my father had not wanted to go back to Africa, his goal had been to build from *within* Jamaica. He was not going to beg for money for repatriation, and he would tell people: "Build your own society—you can! You have done it for thousands of years: you built Egypt, you built the USA, you have it within you. Everything you want to achieve, you can do, just believe in yourself and believe in your people." The fact is, Rasta is now one of the largest Black social movements in the world—and it's less than a hundred years old.

ABI Reggae was an amazing event, and my wife and I couldn't believe the reception we received. We were treated like royalty: we stayed in a beautiful hotel and were provided a chauffeur-driven car for our personal use. I, especially, was treated like a rock star. I was recognized in the streets, thanks to Hélène Lee's documentary *The First Rasta*, based on her book, in which I appeared; everyone wanted to have their picture taken with me. High school students came to hear me speak, and I was later mobbed by them, while some schoolgirls asked permission to take pictures with my wife. Never in my life have I signed so many autographs. The only problem was that I didn't speak French, though some spoke enough English to make communication possible.

All of this was motivated by a deep love and respect for Leonard Howell, a man who in his own country had been persecuted, imprisoned, sent to a psychiatric hospital, financially and socially ruined, and even now continues to be cheated of his legacy. A man who gave a gift to the world and was tormented for the rest of his life. Rastafari and reggae were born in Jamaica, and now a foreign country whose language I didn't even speak was proudly promoting Dada's vision.

Curlyn and I were impressed by the level of knowledge among the dignitaries from other African countries. We felt at home in the presence of Horace Campbell, a Jamaican professor at Syracuse University with a vast knowledge of my father, and we were introduced to historian Giulia Bonacci, author of a book on Shashemene. For the first time, I met Mutabaruka, a Jamaican poet, singer, intellectual, and radio personality whose shows I often listened to, and whose wife, Jacqueline Spence, had been a classmate of Curlyn's at Wolmer's Girls School. One of our most memorable encounters was with the thundering

Ijahnya, grandniece of Robert Athlyi Rogers, author of *The Holy Piby,* a document issued in the 1920s which had inspired my father. All of these people have contributed to Rasta in one way or another, and at ABI Reggae, we all felt as one arrow, aiming in the same direction—and it was the very first time we'd had occasion to do so.

In the global context of discrimination against the Rastas, the ABI Reggae festival was a daring endeavor. Yet there is no doubt that Rasta has been a positive force throughout Africa. Since the 1980s, for example, reggae has been one of the most popular musical genres in the Ivory Coast. Hundreds of musicians have become the voices for a younger generation. I hope this generation will be curious enough to explore the manyfold aspects of our heritage, move beyond the clichés and mass manipulation, and find there some food for thought and hopefully some teachings for the future. Rasta is still being defined—and Africa will play a critical role in this.

To the many groups, students, and people I have spoken to, I send my greetings and encouragement. Yes, we can do it! Roar like a lion and build the world anew!

AFTERWORD

‖‖‖

Rasta, like all things in life, shall evolve and adapt. But it is important not to lose touch with the original vision. Groups with no ties or connections to Pinnacle are still trying to coax the Jamaican government to include them in matters relating to Pinnacle and Rasta. Some of these new Rastas are speaking in the name of my father, claiming his land, trying to insinuate themselves into his heritage, but they have nothing to do with Pinnacle and know nothing about it. They make absurd statements, referring to things like a "second dispensation of the emperor." Some fly our Rasta flag upside down. But try as they might, they cannot change history.

In early 2000, a group of people attemped to hijack the leadership of Rasta. Their leader claimed he was one of Leonard Howell's sons and had been "elected" to represent all Rastas. None of us Howell children were aware of what was happening until Michael Boyd, one of my father's mentees from Tredegar Park, got in touch with our family. (One of the many fond childhood memories Michael shared with us of his encounters with Dada was the way in which he would stoop to be eye level with a child to whom he was speaking. It was a small gesture of respect that resonated greatly.)

In 2005, the Leonard P. Howell Foundation was established by the Howell family and close associates, with the goal of teaching future generations about the true legacy of Leonard Howell, Pinnacle, and Rasta.

In honor of my father's influential movement and all of the loved ones we buried in that paradise, especially my mother, the LPH Foundation and my family have been trying for years to persuade the Ministry of Culture, Gender, Entertainment and Sport (and its predecessor), as well as the Jamaican National Heritage Trust, to declare certain plots of Pinnacle as a National Heritage Site. Unfortunately, "justice" has meant handing down unfavorable decisions made by accomplices and politicians on both sides of the political divide without much regard for Dada's legacy, the dead who we buried, or the way we were all pushed out.

On October 17, 2022, the government of Jamaica posthumously awarded Leonard Howell the Order of Distinction in the rank of "Officer," "for pioneering the development of the Rastafarian philosophy." While standing in a tent set up at King's House to receive the medal and scroll on behalf of my father, I had conflicting feelings. This was the first time since 1946 that the Jamaican government had publicly recognized Dada as the founding father of Rasta. I wondered what Dada would have done if he were still alive. Would he have magnanimously accepted the award from the government that once destroyed his life's work, or would he have rejected it? It takes courage to recognize one's mistakes or wrongdoings, and the whole Rasta community along with my family hailed the award as a symbol of the progress the Jamaican government has made in recognizing and understanding the Rasta movement. But was it enough?

The number of lies and cover-ups related to the land title for Pinnacle is astounding, and if someone with significant financial resources and influence is ever able to uncover the truth, I have faith that reparations will follow. The Howell family is united in the dream of one day being able to restore that big house and its surrounding areas to their former glory. Until that day, the legacy of Pinnacle lives on in our hearts.

This book is dedicated to my mother, Tenneth Bent-Howell, who is buried at Pinnacle, and this partial list of the thousands of people and their descendants who lived there:

Abby Lake
Abdul Sutherland
Adassa Copeland-McFarlane
Albert Lewis
Alfred Gallimore
Alva Allen
Andrew J. McFarlane
Arnell Howell
Aston Scott
Audrey Lewis
Augustus MacFarlane
Azeril MacFarlane
Barrington Levine
Berryl Fairweather
Bobby Ward
Canute Swaby
Cardiff Howell
Caroline Dick
Casette Howell
Catherine Howell
Cera Powell
Charles Scott
Christine Black
Clement Gardener
Daphne Howell
Delvieta Simpson
Donavon (Jahdan) Barnes
Dulce Barrett
Edna Black
Enoch Powell
Esmine Thomas
Ethlyn Niklass
Eva Allen
Florence Steward
Garth Alphanso-Howell
George Vancole Fletcher
Gerald (Bunny) Downer
Gilbert McFarlane
Hadly Black
Herman March
Hopeton Swaby
Hortense Barrett
Howard McFarlane
Hyacinth Brown
Hyacinth McKenzie
Icient Bango
Inez Howell
Ivy Sutherland

Jim Howell
Junior Wisdom
Kevin Anthony-Young Howell
Laurel Marsh
Leonard Bailey
Lester Powell
Lloyd Copeland
Louis Campbell
Lovelace MacFarlane
Lovie Campbell
Lovie Fairweather
Lowie Campbell
May White
Megan Block
Melvin McFarlane
Merriman Barrett
Mindell Sutherland
Monica Valentine
Monty Howell
Myrtle Howell
Nevlyn Morris
Noel Barrett
Norman Marsh
Olive Malave
Omar K. Maragh
Patrick Howell
Pearl Staniger
Perry Bailey
Peter Johnson
Peter Thomas
Phillip Brown
Ras Lion
Remy Howell
Rodriquez Anderson
Roslyn Valentine
Sebert Walker
Septimus Gilimore
Seymour Bailey
Shedrock Pryce
Steve McFarlane
Terry Howell
Tilly Black
Toot Barrett
Virginia White
Zanas Sutherland
Zodia Howell

Acknowledgments

I am grateful for the hard work, dedication, and support of all the people who have helped spread my father's legacy, including (in no particular order): Hélène Lee for thirty years of dedicated work and love; Michael Boyd for keeping the faith throughout the decades; Jacqueline Duclaud, Ras Miguel Lorne, Clinton Hutton, Bongo Niah, Michael Barnett, Robert Bond, Dr. K'adamawi K'nife, Dr. D.A. Dunkley, Clyde McKenzie, Stephen Golding, Elaine Wint, Roger Steffens, Jakes Homiak, Doctor Dread, Patrick Howell, and Ingrid "Sister Hodash" McLean Robinson.

Many thanks to Sister Fan'aye SunLight Selassie, who has tirelessly built the LPH Foundation website; Ras Kahleb and Donisha Prendergast for the Occupy Pinnacle Movement; Dr. Louis E.A. Moyston, who was one of the first scholars to publicly recognize my father as the founder of Rasta; and Gabriel Alexander—beyond being family, you have been a helping friend through and through.

And to all of my brothers and sisters who Dada gave me: Zodie, Myrtle, Jim, Remy, Enid, Inez, and especially Monty and Katherine for being on the front lines of the LPH Foundation with me.

The list of supporters continues to grow . . .

Crime still on. The Minister said that many guns are still out there in the hands of dangerous criminals with nine out of the 12 most wanted men still at large." In view of such considerations the minister said Operation Crime Stop must continue.

The evil liars used to say that ganja which comes from God caused a person to do evil, to do the devils works. Or it would make you mad or make you crave hard drugs.

now They know that the people won't believe this garbage and lies anymore. They know that none of these things happened that were supposed to happen if you use herbs new more wicked approch by blasphemer know nothings

Anyone who dares to be so presumptuous as to tell lies about ganja a male and female herb Better not complain when all the sick people start throwing stones and broken bottles at you when they realize that you tried to make them slaves to Bablonian society and strangers to the ganja filled kingdom of the Most High. That you filled them with chemicals and cancer and death while God had prepared herbs holiness and life. Ganja users are secure in their knowledge that ganja is a male and female herb bearing seeds that our God has freely given us.

Handwritten by Leonard P. Howell in 1981. All his life, Howell read sacred and secular books, newspapers, leaflets, and encyclopedias, some of which he acquired abroad. He also kept notes and copied articles that interested him into his notebook. His library and his notes all disappeared during the multiple raids and shakedowns; all that remains is his notebook from the final months of his life.